FRANCIS FRITH'S

ST ALBANS - A HISTORY AND CELEBRATION

THE FRANCIS FRITH COLLECTION

www.francisfrith.com

ST ALBANS

A HISTORY AND CELEBRATION
OF THE CITY

TOM DOIG

THE FRANCIS FRITH COLLECTION

www.francisfrith.com

First published in the United Kingdom in 2004
by The Francis Frith Collection®

Hardback edition 2004 ISBN 1-90493-845-0
Paperback edition 2012 ISBN 978-1-84589-652-2

British Library Cataloguing in Publication Data

St Albans - A History and Celebration of the City
Tom Doig

The Francis Frith Collection®
Oakley Business Park, Wylye Road,
Dinton, Wiltshire SP3 5EU
Tel: +44 (0) 1722 716 376
Email: info@francisfrith.co.uk
www.francisfrith.com

Printed and bound in Great Britain
Contains material sourced from responsibly managed forests

Front Cover: **ST ALBANS, CHEQUER STREET 1921** 70481t

Additional photographs by Tom Doig.

Domesday extract used in timeline by kind permission of
Alecto Historical Editions, www.domesdaybook.org
Aerial photographs reproduced under licence from
Simmons Aerofilms Limited.
Historical Ordnance Survey maps reproduced under licence from
Homecheck.co.uk

Every attempt has been made to contact copyright holders of
illustrative material. We will be happy to give full acknowledgement in
future editions for any items not credited. Any information should be
directed to The Francis Frith Collection.

*The colour-tinting in this book is for illustrative purposes only,
and is not intended to be historically accurate*

AS WITH ANY HISTORICAL DATABASE, THE FRANCIS FRITH ARCHIVE IS
CONSTANTLY BEING CORRECTED AND IMPROVED, AND THE PUBLISHERS
WOULD WELCOME INFORMATION ON OMISSIONS OR INACCURACIES

Contents

ST ALBANS, FROM THE AIR 1935 AF47108

Historical Timeline for St Albans

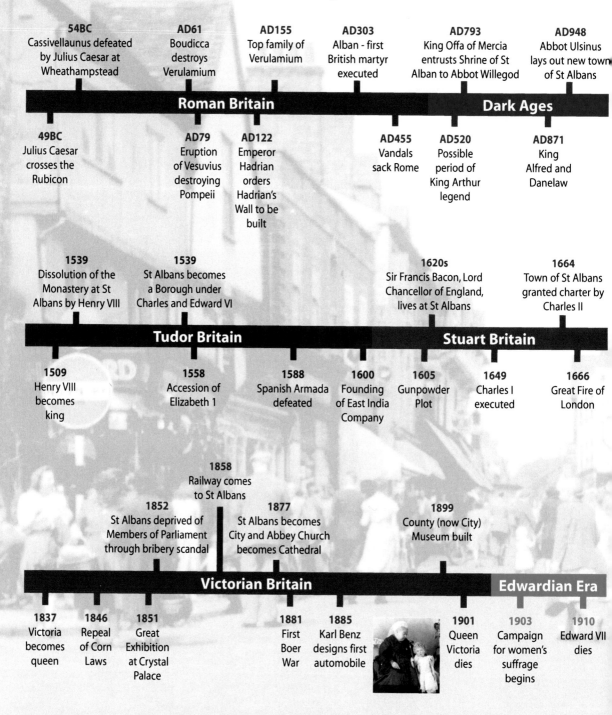

54BC
Cassivellaunus defeated
by Julius Caesar at
Wheathampstead

AD61
Boudicca
destroys
Verulamium

AD155
Top family of
Verulamium

AD303
Alban - first
British martyr
executed

AD793
King Offa of Mercia
entrusts Shrine of St
Alban to Abbot Willegod

AD948
Abbot Ulsinus
lays out new town
of St Albans

Roman Britain | **Dark Ages**

49BC
Julius Caesar
crosses the
Rubicon

AD79
Eruption
of Vesuvius
destroying
Pompeii

AD122
Emperor
Hadrian
orders
Hadrian's
Wall to be
built

AD455
Vandals
sack Rome

AD520
Possible
period of
King Arthur
legend

AD871
King
Alfred and
Danelaw

1539
Dissolution of the
Monastery at St
Albans by Henry VIII

1539
St Albans becomes
a Borough under
Charles and Edward VI

1620s
Sir Francis Bacon, Lord
Chancellor of England,
lives at St Albans

1664
Town of St Albans
granted charter by
Charles II

Tudor Britain | **Stuart Britain**

1509
Henry VIII
becomes
king

1558
Accession of
Elizabeth 1

1588
Spanish Armada
defeated

1600
Founding
of East India
Company

1605
Gunpowder
Plot

1649
Charles I
executed

1666
Great Fire of
London

1858
Railway comes
to St Albans

1852
St Albans deprived of
Members of Parliament
through bribery scandal

1877
St Albans becomes
City and Abbey Church
becomes Cathedral

1899
County (now City)
Museum built

Victorian Britain | **Edwardian Era**

1837
Victoria
becomes
queen

1846
Repeal
of Corn
Laws

1851
Great
Exhibition
at Crystal
Palace

1881
First
Boer
War

1885
Karl Benz
designs first
automobile

1901
Queen
Victoria
dies

1903
Campaign
for women's
suffrage
begins

1910
Edward VII
dies

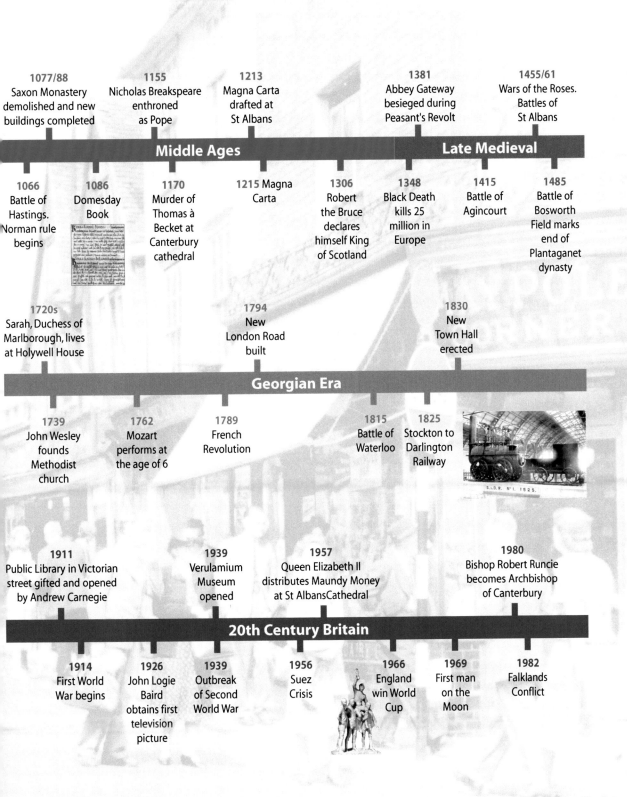

1077/88 Saxon Monastery demolished and new buildings completed

1155 Nicholas Breakspeare enthroned as Pope

1213 Magna Carta drafted at St Albans

1381 Abbey Gateway besieged during Peasant's Revolt

1455/61 Wars of the Roses. Battles of St Albans

Middle Ages

Late Medieval

1066 Battle of Hastings. Norman rule begins

1086 Domesday Book

1170 Murder of Thomas à Becket at Canterbury cathedral

1215 Magna Carta

1306 Robert the Bruce declares himself King of Scotland

1348 Black Death kills 25 million in Europe

1415 Battle of Agincourt

1485 Battle of Bosworth Field marks end of Plantaganet dynasty

1720s Sarah, Duchess of Marlborough, lives at Holywell House

1794 New London Road built

1830 New Town Hall erected

Georgian Era

1739 John Wesley founds Methodist church

1762 Mozart performs at the age of 6

1789 French Revolution

1815 Battle of Waterloo

1825 Stockton to Darlington Railway

S.&D.R. Nº1. 1825.

1911 Public Library in Victorian street gifted and opened by Andrew Carnegie

1939 Verulamium Museum opened

1957 Queen Elizabeth II distributes Maundy Money at St AlbansCathedral

1980 Bishop Robert Runcie becomes Archbishop of Canterbury

20th Century Britain

1914 First World War begins

1926 John Logie Baird obtains first television picture

1939 Outbreak of Second World War

1956 Suez Crisis

1966 England win World Cup

1969 First man on the Moon

1982 Falklands Conflict

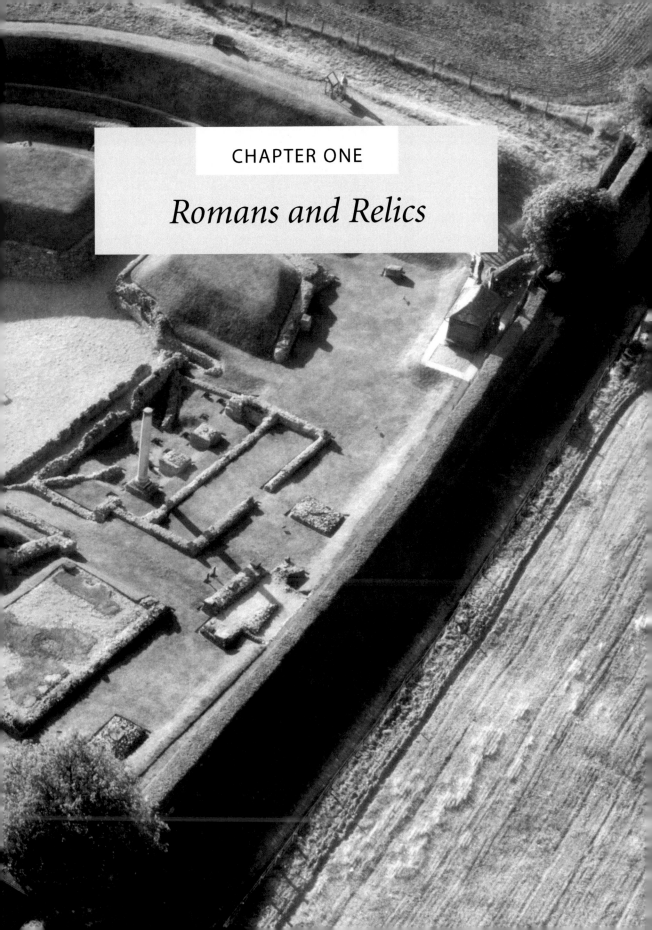

CHAPTER ONE

Romans and Relics

'Let's go to St Albans - nice quiet place, St Albans.'

Three Men in a Boat (1889) - Jerome K Jerome

HERTFORDSHIRE'S CATHEDRAL city is famed for its connection with the Roman occupation and the nearby Roman town of Verulamium. However St Albans is more than just a museum piece. It is a living city which brings together a busy business community with many old and historic buildings and streets.

The town of St Albans took its name from Alban, a British-born saint and martyr of the third century, the story of whose conversion to Christianity by a wandering priest, whom he had sheltered, is told by the Venerable Bede. He writes:

'AD 305, the blessed Alban suffered death on the 22nd June, near the city of Verulam, where afterwards, when peaceable Christian times were restored, a church of wonderful workmanship, and suitable to his martyrdom, was erected'.

The written story of St Albans spans almost two thousand years. Although the earliest documentation dates from Roman times, the history of the locality can be traced

THE CATHEDRAL AND ABBEY CHURCH 2004 S2730k (Tom Doig)

back through the warm periods between successive ice ages. A tantalising glimpse into early human habitation is offered by the few flint hand tools discovered at Flamstead End manufactured by early Stone Age man. Before the Romans came the principal regional centre of the local Celtic tribe was first at Wheathampstead, then the hilltop of Prae Wood, overlooking the Ver valley and at that period heavily forested. This could be the well-fortified stronghold that Caesar refers to in his 'De Bello Gallico' where he says that in 54BC he overcame Cassivellaunus, king of the Catuvellauni tribe. By the time of the great Roman invasion of 43AD, Iron Age Verulamium was a thriving town and within a few years it was raised to the status of 'municipium,' an honour which was not awarded to any other city in Roman Britain.

The Romans, when they established themselves in Britain after AD43, built the first Verulamium down the hillside from Prae Wood - Bluehouse Hill it is called today - towards the Ver, where it protected a ford; this first Verulamium was overrun during the insurrection of Boudicca in AD61 and many of the inhabitants were slaughtered but, on the defeat of the British queen, the city quickly recovered and was rebuilt. A hundred years after, the city was destroyed by fire and again rebuilt, but this time in stone and to a very high standard. Many of the buildings had underfloor central heating systems known as 'hypocausts' and one of these can still be seen today in a special display pavilion in Verulamium Park. The city of over 200 acres was surrounded by a defensive wall

A RECONSTRUCTION OF AN IRON AGE ROUNDHOUSE
ZZZ01297 (Reproduced by kind permission of the Ancient Technology Centre, Cranborne, Dorset)

over two miles long and, it is thought, had a triumphal arch close to the south gate. There were numerous temples and civic buildings including the Basilica, said to have been St Alban's last resting place before he was led to his execution.

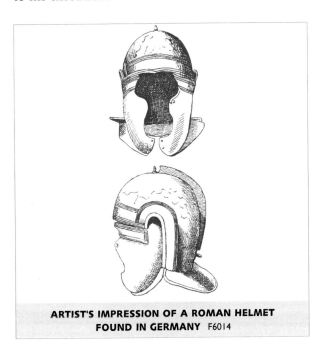

ARTIST'S IMPRESSION OF A ROMAN HELMET FOUND IN GERMANY F6014

THE CAUSEWAY 1921 70483

The Causeway leads from St Germain's Gate at the bottom of Abbey Mill Lane along the Saxon embankment past the remains of the Roman wall. The embankment was originally part of the bank splitting the upper and lower fishponds. Following the Causeway along the Saxon rampart from St Germain's gate at the bottom of Abbey Mill Lane we come to the edge of the Roman town of Verulamium.

North of the centre of the city stood the Theatre. Excavated in the 1930s, this was found to have seated about 1600 spectators and was used for plays, readings and, probably, civic meetings. The area around the Theatre has also been thoroughly investigated and surveyed; a broad range of artefacts have been carefully conserved and are on display in the excellent Verulamium Museum opposite to St Michael's Church.

When the Romans left Britain in the fifth century, Verulamium fell into decay and it became an enormous 'reclamation centre'

where the materials were used to construct the Abbey, churches and other buildings in the new town of St Albans which was starting to flourish nearby.

It is difficult, even impossible, to identify the exact date of the founding of the holy place at St Albans. At a date traditionally said to be AD303 but, as has lately been argued, possibly a century earlier, the martyrdom of St Alban was followed shortly afterwards by the erection of a shrine on the hilltop where he was said to have suffered death by beheading. In 429, two French bishops - the

THE ROMAN THEATRE c1959 S2159

Bishop of Auxerre (later to be beatified as Saint Germanus) and the Bishop of Troyes - came to the shrine of St Alban. A synod had been called to settle the problem of Pelagius, whose radical and possibly heretical teaching was threatening to cause a theological rift. These bishops were probably the first recorded visitors to the shrine.

Rudolph Robert, in 'Hertfordshire Countryside' of Autumn 1963, says that in 793, Offa, King of Mercia, overlord of all England and self-styled 'rex Anglicorum', laid the foundation stone of a Benedictine monastery on the site of a small church near the location of the shrine. One of the Abbots was Ulsinus who, in 948, founded the market and has been attributed with establishing the three churches on the main roads to the town.

St Stephen's Hill, at the southern end of Holywell Hill where it meets Watling Street, takes its name from the wooden steepled St Stephen's Church, one of the three founded by Abbot Ulsinus at the entrances to the town around 948. Built on the site of a Roman cemetery, it prospered from its position as the first church to greet pilgrims on their way from London before the long grind up the hill to the Shrine of St Alban.

Here, the pilgrims would have been absolved of their sins by the priest in preparation for entering the Holy Abbey. The Lady Chapel dates from the 13th century and was originally used for worship by the male lepers who lived at the adjacent St Julian's Chapel, founded around 1130 by Geoffrey de Goram. When the Chapel and the Church were linked, a 'squint' was driven through the wall so that the lepers could witness the services.

Today, visitors are greeted by a message beautifully carved and painted and mounted

ST STEPHEN'S CHURCH ZZZ01726

below the clock. It reads 'I that please some, try all.' Maybe not so direct as the motif from Furneux Pelham Church, in north east Hertfordshire, which reminds us 'Time flies. Mind your Business', but still timely enough. In early times, crossing the River Ver had been a major difficulty, particularly in the winter when the river was swollen and the banks almost impassably swampy. In 1143, a bridge was built to provide a safe and dry crossing and, at the same time, in view of the unrest caused by the dispute between King Stephen and his cousin, the Empress Matilda, new defensive ditches around the town were built and existing ones improved.

St Michael's Church is another that was founded by Abbot Ulsinus. Located at the western entrance to the St Albans, it stands on the site of part of the Roman forum and is, indeed, built from its remains. As well as the Roman brick, tile and flint walls, the Saxon windows and Norman arches are surrounded by the plundered remains from Verulamium.

The original St Michael's Church was much smaller than the present structure. It probably comprised just a chancel and a nave. During the Norman period, the north and south aisles were added but, it appears, not a tower. This seems to have been a later addition.

On the south-east corner of the outside of the chancel there is a small niche which may have been the cell of an anchoress. Like St Peter's at around the same time, there certainly was one of these solitary holy women living at St Michael's in 1486 for according to Susan Flood's, 'St Albans Wills

1471-1500', Dame Constance Cressy left 'to the Ancress of Seint Michell, 3s 4d.' But did she use the niche to beg for alms and pray for the souls of the deceased? There is no positive evidence.

One of the earliest mentions in writing of St Michael's can be found in a record of about 1180 when the relics of Alban were carried along the road to Gorhambury past the church. Rosemary Woodland, in her article in 'Hertfordshire Countryside' of March 2003, tells us that the procession was met by one bearing the bones of St Amphibalus and they were combined to return to the Abbey. A manuscript written in AD209 at Auxerre says that Alban, a Romano-Briton had sheltered Amphibalus, a Christian priest who was fleeing from his persecutors. Alban was converted to Christianity by him. When the soldiers searched his house, Alban helped the priest to escape by exchanging clothes. For this, and for refusing to acknowledge the Roman gods, Alban was executed.

It is claimed that, in Saxon times, when workmen were gathering material from the ruins of Verulamium, they came across a collection of books and manuscripts on the story of Alban, written in the ancient British dialect. The documents were translated into Latin by a monk called Unwona. As soon as the work was completed, the originals crumbled to dust. Geoffrey of Monmouth, the Welsh historian working in the early 1100s, retold the story in his 'Historia Regum Britannica' but managed to misinterpret the Latin phrase containing the word 'Amphibalus.' He assumed it was the name of the Christian priest - actually it is the word for the disguise he was given by Alban, an outer jacket. So, for all these years, we have been venerating St Overcoat!

In 1178, Robert Mercer had a dream where St Alban showed him the burial place of Amphibalus on Redbourn Heath, just outside the town. When the Abbot got to hear of it, he arranged an expedition to excavate the Mounds of the Banners. Ten skeletons were found and one was 'positively' identified as Amphibalus. The remains of Alban were brought to meet Amphibalus - this was the dual procession recorded in 1180. At the place where the two processions met, a women's leper hospital called St Mary de Pre was founded in 1190. It closed in 1528 but the remains are possibly those that can still be traced during drought near Prea Wood on the road to Gorhambury.

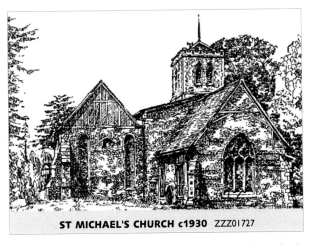

ST MICHAEL'S CHURCH c1930 ZZZ01727

This small church at the entrance to St Albans dates back to Saxon times. Much of the fabric, however, comes from the Roman city of Verulamium. St Michael's was extensively restored by Lord Grimthorp in 1898, but, fortunately, most of the early features have survived.

THE ABBEY, THE SHRINE OF AMPHIBALUS c1885
18056

The shrine of St Amphibalus was built by Abbot William of Trumpington to hold the relics of the saint and the bones of his 'companions'.

Abbot William of Trumpington had a special affection for Amphibalus and gathered relics from all over the country. In order to house them, and the remains of the skeletons that were discovered with him, he extended and moved the shrine to the centre of the Abbey from its original home at Redbourn. On 10th October 1323, two of the south nave columns collapsed bringing with them part of the roof and cloisters. The shrine was badly damaged and all but destroyed. It was said that through the intervention of St Amphibalus none of those attending mass were injured. As a token of thanksgiving, Ralph de Whitechurche gifted a new shrine which was built using some of the original material.

A NORMAN SHIP F6019

The Roman town of Verulamium was bought by the ecclesiastical authorities in 1005. Paul of Caen, a Norman and, 'rigid and prudent in the observance of the religious order,' was appointed Abbot in 1077, and he set about building the new Abbey using materials from the abandoned Roman town and pillars from the Saxon church.

The body of the Abbey, rendered with plaster and painted white was completed within 11 years. Much of the outer buildings were built to a standard design and dimension and constructed from Totternhoe limestone. They comprised cloisters, a chapel, a dormitory, an infirmary and a garden. Further down the hill, another group of buildings included a chapter house, a common room, a refectory, granaries, a kitchen and a larder. There was also a block with an audience chamber and royal apartments for the use of important visitors. A bakehouse, a brewhouse and a buttery provided the Abbey community with most of its requirements in the way of food and drink. Finally, there was accommodation within the bounds of the monastery for guests and travellers, and stabling for 200 horses.

Further work was carried out to extend the Abbey by Abbot John de Cella but financial difficulties meant that the work had to be put in abeyance. Towards the end of his tenure as Abbot, in 1213, John hosted a grand assembly of barons, knights, bishops and sheriffs at St Albans. King John had refused to recognise Stephen Langton as Archbishop of Canterbury and, apart from changes to common law which

had been implemented without consulting them, the barons were afraid of being excommunicated by Rome. The result of the assembly was the drafting of what we know as Magna Carta.

John de Cella did not live to see Magna Carta signed by King John in 1215 for he died late in 1213. The following year, in 1214, Abbot William de Trumpington was appointed and, under the new regime, eventually completed the work including the erection of an octagonal leaded spire. This survived into the early 16th century when it was replaced with a short and stubby 'Hertfordshire spike.' (This was finally removed in May 1833.)

Three years later, in 1217, a young novice who had passed through the Abbey School was accepted as a monk. Probably one of the best known monks to be associated with St Albans, Matthew Paris, 'the universal genius,' became a scribe and wrote one of the earliest histories of England and produced one of the earliest maps of Britain, which are preserved in the British Museum. His knowledge of the history of the Abbey estate was invaluable and his recorded inventories of the contents are unique in this country.

Pilgrims would have travelled here with one sole purpose - to visit the shrine of St Alban. Miracles were reported to have taken place here and Shakespeare mentions one in Henry VI when the Duke of Suffolk asks about miracles and a local inhabitant replies: 'Forsooth, a blind man at St Alban's shrine within this half-hour hath received his sight; a man that ne'er saw his life before.'

A MEDIEVAL KNIGHT AND HIS LADY, FROM A TOMB IN INGHAM CHURCH, NORFOLK F6018

THE SHRINE OF ST ALBAN AND THE WATCHING CHAMBER c1960 S2117

Pilgrims hoping for forgiveness and miraculous cures flocked to the shrine of St Alban. Gifts would have been placed in the diamond shaped orifices whilst the monks in the Watching Chamber made sure they did not take away more than they gave!

The original shrine was in three sections. The lower part was of Purbeck marble with a clunch canopy. It had small niches and holes through which the pilgrims placed their offerings. Above this was a plinth supporting the casket which contained the bones and relics of Alban. This was removable and could be carried on the shoulders of the monks during religious processions. Finally there was a (probably wooden) cover which could be raised and lowered by means of a rope and pulley. There is a hole high up in the vaulting roof to accommodate the mechanism. It was broken up into over 1000 pieces in 1539 at the dissolution and the shattered parts were used to block up a doorway. The remains were discovered during the restoration in 1872 and the shrine was reassembled, on the base which had survived, and installed in its original location. However, in 1993, the glue that had been used during the reconstruction was found to have deteriorated and the shrine was in danger of collapse. At a cost of £150,000 the shrine was restored for a second time and the protective iron railings refurbished. The shrine, although empty for the relics are said to have been stolen by Danish monks in Saxon times, continues

to attract pilgrims from all over the world including young people from the Diocesan Youth Pilgrimage which was started in 1946.

Overlooking the Shrine of St Alban, the wooden Watching Gallery was used by the monks to keep a constant vigil, no doubt, to ensure that pilgrims did not chip away

THE WATCHING CHAMBER 1960 19464

The monks of St Albans kept a wary eye on the pilgrims visiting the shrine of the saint from this wooden two-storey chamber.

fragments as souvenirs. It was built, around 1400, under a bequest of 20 shillings set up by Robert of Malton. The chamber, which was looked after by the Custos Feretri, survived the dissolution although changing fortunes and time have reduced its splendid, colourful facade to the naked oak of today. On the outside, the Gallery is carved with panels representing the months and the martyrdom of St Alban. A final panel contains the arms of King Richard III. The door to the Gallery opens onto a small room and a short heavy staircase to the upper floor. In one of the exterior doors, there is a small slot to receive coins from the pilgrims - the remains of the leather collecting pouch still survive behind it. On the ground floor are a number of cupboards which would have held holy relics and the larger and more valuable gifts from the pilgrims. Upstairs there are eight open panels which give a fine view over the Shrine and the Custos, who was responsible for

ensuring the security of the Abbey's relics and treasures as well as controlling and guiding the vast number of visitors, would be able to keep a watchful eye on the proceedings.

The Black Death of 1349 killed almost one third of the population of England and swept through the Abbey taking many of the monks and the Abbot. The new Abbot was Thomas

---

Did you know?

The Only English Pope

Around 1100, a Nicholas Breakspeare was born at nearby Abbots Langley. When he was a lad, his father abandoned him to become a monk and his only course of action was to follow his father and take the cowl. It is said that he attended the monastery school at St Albans but failed to be accepted into holy orders. After travelling to France he was accepted by the monastery of St Rufus near Avignon. Called to Rome, his ability was instantly recognised and he was elected Pope Adrian IV in 1154. Five years later, he died at Rome. He was the first, and so far the only, English Pope.

---

de la Mere who had the Gatehouse built. He lived to the great age of 87 years and died in 1396. Thomas lived to see the Peasants' Revolt of 1381, when John Ball was imprisoned, hanged, drawn and quartered at Romeland opposite the Abbey Gatehouse. Ball was an excommunicated priest who had preached that the church should embrace poverty and that all people should be socially equal.

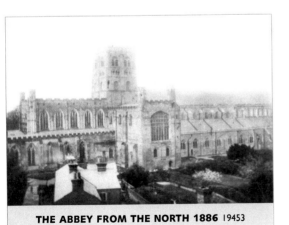

THE ABBEY FROM THE NORTH 1886 19453

A unique view of the Abbey prior to the restorations of the 1880s. The photograph was taken from the north, possibly from the top of the Clock Tower.

This was totally unacceptable and at his trial the ecclesiastical judges asserted that the Abbot ruled under the government of the King. As these ecclesiastical judges were appointed by the Abbot, the outcome of the trial was a foregone conclusion. During the same revolt, on 14th June, Wat Tyler and Jack Straw 'with an army of rebels' marched from Barnet to St Albans and, with the leaders of the local contingent, William Grindecobbe and John Ball, demanded of de la Mere that he return the charters that had made them serfs. They broke into the Abbey and smashed the parlour floor to retrieve the papers and burned the documents. Richard of Wallingford, one of the major monastic chroniclers, records they were 'passing them out as if they were communion hosts.' Suddenly there began a rumour that Tyler, who had returned to London, had been killed and the crowd dispersed and the leaders fled. Soon afterwards, John Ball was captured at Coventry and brought back to St Albans. Grindecobbe was also caught and was offered his life on condition that he helped pacify the townspeople. He sealed his fate by calling them to 'Hold firm while you can, and have no thought for me or what I may suffer, for if I die in the course of liberty we have won. I think myself happy to end my life as a martyr.' He did die but to no avail. The townspeople were forced to pay £200 for the damage to the abbey, and to give up the liberties that they had extorted from the abbot.

John Bostock of Wheathampstead had two terms as Abbot, from 1420 to 1440 and 1452 to 1465. During his time at Balliol College,

he came to know Humphrey, Duke of Gloucester, the brother of King Henry V. Humphrey was later involved in bitter quarrels with his uncle, Henry Beaufort, Bishop of Winchester, and it is probably because of this that he was denied burial in Westminster Abbey. John Bostock stepped in and, when he died in 1447, Humphrey was interred in St Albans Abbey. When the tomb was discovered in the Abbey, by chance, in 1703 it was found that the body had been preserved in a 'brown liquor pickle of a highly aromatic smell which so many were curious to taste ....very unwisely people dip their fingers in the liquor to endeavour to find what it is made of.' In 1854, Ford Maddox Brown visited St Albans and went to see the remains of the Duke. 'It might have been anyone else for all we could tell, but we took it on trust.'

One of the last abbots before the dissolution was William of Wallingford. He had the great high altar screen erected in 1484 but, despite its richness, this was desecrated after the Reformation and the original statues which filled the niches were stolen (see pages 24-25). William had a window built in the north transept which was replaced by the Rose Window during the Victorian restoration. He also installed a window in the south transept which was destroyed in a storm in 1703. All trace of it was removed during Lord Grimthorpe's renovations in the 19th century.

At the eastern end of the south side of the High Street, snug between shops is the entrance to Waxhouse Gate. The Gate was almost opposite the Clock Tower and the footpath leading to Market Place. There is a suggestion that there was an earlier gate built in 1420 and removed in 1722 - its outline might be seen in the frame to an adjacent shop window. The Gate was built at the entrance to a narrow street, leading to the Abbey, where beeswax candles, a by-product of the traditional monk's occupation as bee keeper, were manufactured for pilgrims to burn at the Shrine of the Saint at the Abbey. Clearly the people in the 16th century had a stronger constitution than those later residents who complained about the smell from the tallow factory owned by Edward Sutton Wiles in the 19th century (see Chapter Three).

In 1535 the small monasteries, those worth less than £200 per annum, were closed by order of King Henry VIII, whilst the larger establishments such as St Albans survived until December 1539 when the Great Seal was passed to the representatives of King Henry VIII as 'The Supreme Head of the Church of England.' At that moment, St Albans felt the full force of the dissolution of the monasteries.

THE ABBEY GATEWAY c1955 S2069

It is difficult to imagine that this peaceful place was once the site of the country's greatest riot. Long before the French Revolution, England in 1381 suffered the Peasant's Revolt, and the Gateway was stormed by the mob as they prepared to break into the Abbey to retrieve the suppressive charters.

The Wallingford Screen

Installed a few decades before the dissolution by Abbot William of Wallingford, this magnificent screen survived the dissolution but was subsequently vandalised and the statues stolen.

The present statues on the high altar screen are replacements installed by Lord Aldenham in the 1890s. The reredos bass relief of the Resurrection of Christ was sculpted from marble and New Zealand paua shell by Sir Alfred Gilbert. The screen is almost without parallel in this country with the exception of that at Winchester which is slightly smaller. St Alban can be seen in the niche to the right of the Resurrection reredos. Further right, in the lower niche is St Chad. His day is recalled in the Hertfordshire weather lore poem:

First comes David, next comes Chad,
Then comes Wynnel, blowing like mad!

St David's Day is 1st March, St Chad is celebrated on 2nd March and St Wynnel, patron of the wind and carpenters, is remembered on the 3rd March. Wynnel is the special saint of the author as a small chapel, lost centuries ago, gave the name to his house in north-east Hertfordshire.

THE WALLINGFORD SCREEN AND ALTAR c1960 S2115

THE ABBEY GATEWAY c1955 S2069

ST ALBANS, FROM THE AIR 1939 AFR6148

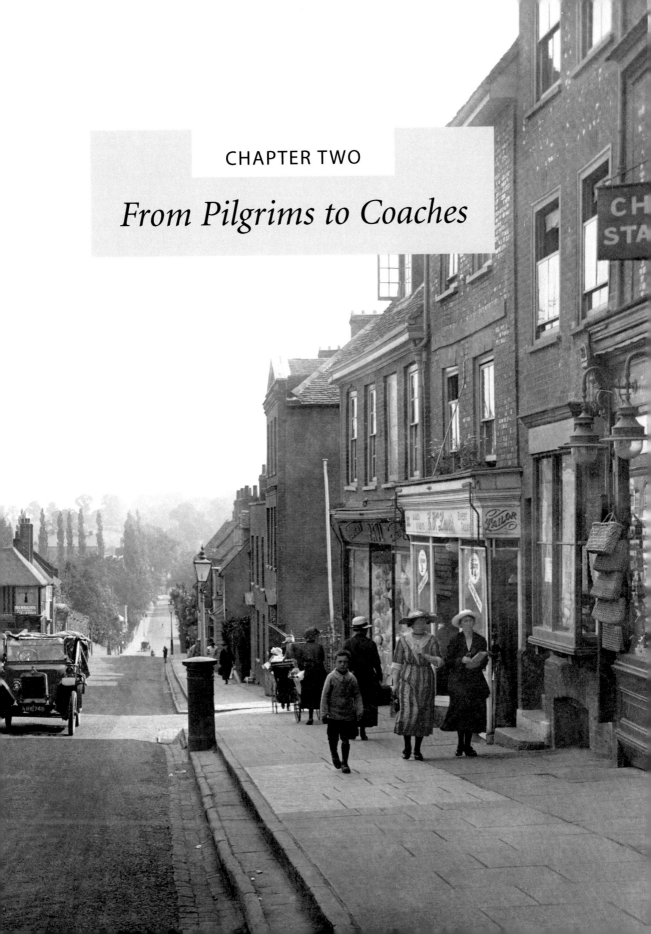

CHAPTER TWO

From Pilgrims to Coaches

THE OLD MONASTERY GATEWAY 1921 70470

All that survives of the original Abbey outbuilding is the Great Gateway. At one time it housed the Grammar School.

AFTER KING EDWARD I's wife, Eleanor, died in Lincolnshire in 1290, her body was brought back to Westminster for burial.

At each of the overnight stopping places - John Shrimpton, the historian says, the Queen's 'dead corps was carried by easie journeyes' - Edward had a Cross erected in her memory. Her 'dead corps' was met at St Michael's by the whole monastic congregation dressed in albs and copes who in 'the most imposing spectacle that England ever witnessed' escorted the bier to the Abbey. The Cross at St Albans, commemorating her resting place in front of the High Altar in the Abbey on 13th December 1290, stood close to the Clock Tower opposite Waxhouse Gate. Although no illustrations survive, it appears that the Eleanor Cross was ornate and highly decorated, similar to the surviving, although heavily restored, example at Waltham Cross in Hertfordshire. During religious processions, a figure of St Alban was rested here and not allowed to move on until the abbot, tapping it with his crozier, chanted, 'Arise, arise, St Alban, and get thee home to thy sanctuary.'

The effigy was hollow and full of a complex mechanism to make its eyes roll and its head nod. Robert Shrimpton, Mayor of St Albans, reminisced that as a boy in the 1540s, he had 'many times crept into the hollow part thereof.'

The crumbling and uncared for remains which served as a market cross were demolished in 1643 although the base survived until 1701 when it, in turn was removed, to make way for the new Market Cross. Work had begun in 1682 when a payment was made for 'setting down six posts about the Cross and work on hewing them and in plan to stop the old mortiss.' The craftsmen were also paid for removing 'five posts or old pieces of timber from the Cross to Roomland.' It seems that the base of the distressed Eleanor Cross had supported a temporary wooden booth under which higglers sold their produce to the townspeople visiting the market.

The new Market Cross comprised an octagonal open structure standing on eight wooden pillars. High on the roof was mounted a gilded figure of Justice. Under the canopy was a huge wooden pump wheel which brought water from a well. In 1810, a horse drawn van crashed into the building and damaged it beyond repair. Although the remains were taken down, the pump wheel survived for a few more years. Today, the modern octagonal building, albeit standing on cast iron columns, in the middle of The Maltings shopping centre, reflects directly this lost feature of St Albans. The site of the Cross is now a welcome resting place for weary visitors with an unusually shaped set of intertwined benches.

To the west of the Clock Tower runs French Row. This narrow street faced onto the stalls and booths that made up the market which had been granted a new charter in 1553 by King Edward VI; these had slowly become

DRAWING OF THE HIGH STREET IN 1600 ZZZ01720

The stump of the Eleanor Cross close to the junction of Market Street and the Vintry (now the High Street) is shown in a plan of about 1600. On the left is Waxhouse Gate with the Great Red Lion on French Row.

permanent buildings by 1335. The alleys and passages which connect French Row through the Market Place into Chequer Street follow the same lines as the gaps between the original market stalls. French Row had earlier been known as In Vico Francorum, Leathershambles or Leather Market, Cobbler's or Cordwainer's Row - the place where shoes and boots were made and repaired. Cordwainers were said to have originally made shoes from the softest fine leather from Cordova in Spain but later the name changed to refer to all shoe and boot makers. The southern end, by the Clock Tower, was called Women's Market - where traders sold dairy produce such as eggs and butter. The northern end was known as Bocherowe, or Cornchepyng. The Anglo-Saxon word 'chypan' means to sell and evolved into the present day Chipping (as in Chipping Barnet, Chipping Norton, Chipping Sodbury, etc) suggests a market.

THE CLOCK TOWER 2004 S2707k (Tom Doig)

The site of the Eleanor Cross is now a sympathetically designed cobbled public seating area.

THE MALTINGS 2004 S2708k (Tom Doig)

The gazebo in The Maltings Shopping Mall reflects the octagonal Market Cross that once stood in front of the Clock

French Row

FRENCH ROW 1921 70478

There are as many theories as to why this is called French Row as there are people living here! Some say the name goes back to 1217 when French soldiers were billeted here after King John refused to recognise Magna Carta, and 150 years later, in 1356, King John of France was kept prisoner in a house on the site of the Fleur de Lys after the Battle of Poitiers. And then, just before the Magna Carta, an army under Faulkes de Breauté came to St Albans and burnt, murdered, pillaged, etc. All have been suggested for the street being named French Row. 30 years after this photograph was taken, French Row appeared, for a fleeting moment, in the film 'The Money Box'.

FRENCH ROW 2004 S2709k

French Row today. From the 1300s up to the late 1900s public houses and inns lined the sides of French Row offering a range of ales, wines and spirits from all over England and the continent. Today they are mainly coffee houses providing a varied selection of beverages from all over the world.

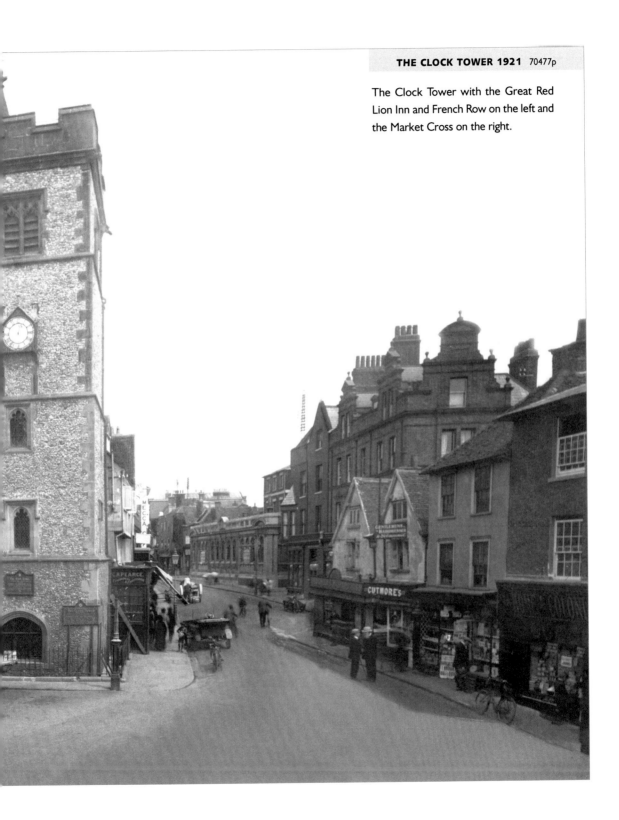

THE CLOCK TOWER 1921 70477p

The Clock Tower with the Great Red Lion Inn and French Row on the left and the Market Cross on the right.

Did you know?

St Albans had a part to play in the Wars of the Roses. On 22nd May 1455, the Lancastrian, Edward Beaufort, Duke of Somerset was killed outside the Castle Inn which stood close to the corner of the present St Peter's Street and Victoria Street. After the battle, the victorious Yorkist troops set about plundering the town although, through bribery rather than diplomacy, the Abbey was spared. The dead were buried in a trench close to St Peter's Street.

The second battle of St Albans, on 17th February 1461, saw a victory for the Lancastrians followed by the now traditional orgy of killing and plundering. The victorious Edward VI reinforced the earlier royal charter and confirmed the Abbey's privileges and its independence from many taxes and laws

Traditionally, on New Year's Day, the stalls and shops sold what were known as Pope Lady cakes. These were small biscuits about five inches in diameter with a head decorated with currant eyes but no arms and legs. Some say that they represented Pope Joan, the female pope who was supposed to have reigned, disguised as a man, from 855 to 859. Others recount the popular and very unlikely legend that a lady and her maids were lost one night near St Albans. Seeing the lights of the town on the top of the hill, they managed to locate the monastery and safety. In gratitude the lady left money for the monks to make and distribute the cakes at the Feast of the Annunciation. The 'dole' came to an end with the dissolution of the monasteries but the local bakers continued the custom, even after the adoption of the revised Gregorian calendar when New Years Day was moved to the first of January.

This fine late medieval house shows all the signs of once having been a shop. The slight jetting and the narrow doorway are typical of the style of shops found in later medieval towns.

FISHPOOL STREET 2004 S2701k (Tom Doig)

Did you know?

One of the buildings on Romeland Hill is said to be haunted. Romeland Cottage was occupied by the family of Francis Skeat, the designer of some of the stained glass in the Cathedral. It seems that a cowled figure, speaking Latin, was seen on a narrow staircase. He wore a strange medallion which glinted in the moonlight. After investigation, it was discovered that the medal was similar to those given to pilgrims at the Abbey as souvenirs and that the Latin was part of a prayer used in earlier times.

The late Geoff Dunk, in his book 'Around St Albans with Geoff Dunk' suggested that it was on the open ground near Butt Lane that 52 men, identified in the Muster Rolls of 1587, gathered to practice their skills with the bow and caliver on the archery butts in preparation for invasion by the Spanish. Although the Armada was defeated in 1588 no one was sure what had happened to the ships that escaped and for five or six years after the men continued to muster waiting for the call to march to Tilbury and defend our shores. It is not recorded how this 'Home Guard' drilled or if any of them had any understanding of what the sea looked like. Indeed, many of them would never have seen a ship larger than a punt on the Ver.

Further along French Row, almost opposite Dagnal Lane, stood the town pillory where summary punishment could be delivered. In 1686 George Field was granted a lease for five butcher's stalls on condition that he erected and maintained a new and substantial pillory. Here also stood a set of stocks but these appear to have been portable and could be sited to maximum advantage. The road to the north of the Dagnal Lane turning became known as Butcher's Row. The discipline in many markets was overseen by what was known as a 'Pye Powder Court' - from the French pied poudre ('dusty feet' of the travellers) and almost certainly such a court existed in St Albans. There is, however, no mention of a pindar whose responsibility it was to look after stray animals and to extract a fee from the owners for their keep in the cattle pound although there was a pound located in what is now Hatfield Road.

Butcher's Row opened out on to St Peter's Street which was lined with shops, inns and better class dwellings. If it were built today, it would be called the Broadway or the Boulevard but from 1275, it has been known by the simple name St Peter's Street. It was originally a huge open market stretching from the Vintry (now High Street) in the south all the way to St Peter's Street in the north. Infilling, particularly at the south, has nibbled away at the boundaries until, by the mid 1880s it reached the shape that we know today.

East of Romeland Hill, the road becomes George Street. This was previously known as Church Street reflecting the church of St Andrew which stood at one time north-west of the Abbey. St Andrews was the parish church until the dissolution but was allowed to fall into disrepair and was eventually cleared around 1630. Of course, after St Andrews, the abbey became the parish church when, in 1553, the burgesses of the town bought it for £400. The Abbey was one of three in Hertfordshire which became parish churches after the dissolution of the monasteries. As well as St Albans, the former priory at Hertford was rebuilt in 1629 and was rededicated to St John the Baptist. At the town of Royston, which had spanned five parishes, the old priory church in 1540, became the church of the newly founded parish.

On the north side of George Street stood The Tabard, The George (whose stable was once converted into a private oratory chapel for those who were too sick to attend Mass at the Abbey) and The Swan, all built around 1400 to provide income for the nuns of Sopwell Priory from visitors to the Abbey. The latter two have now been combined and renamed the Tudor Tavern. This beautifully preserved example of 15th century half-timbering is not only skin deep for the interior is equally attractive with exposed beams, open fire places and uneven timber floors.

The Tabard Inn, later renamed The Antelope, on the corner of Spicer Street was the main Abbey guest house or hostry. It offered accommodation for Abbey retainers and staff - visitors were allowed to stay for only three days - and was supervised by a 'guestmaster' who had an office in Chequer Street. Today part of it provides a different sort of facility for it has been converted into public conveniences!

ST PETER'S STREET 1921 7047lp

CHEQUER STREET 1921   70481p

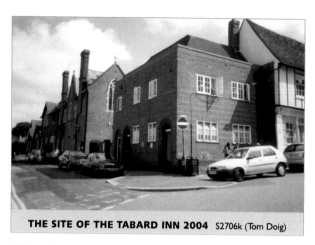

THE SITE OF THE TABARD INN 2004 S2706k (Tom Doig)

Today, the site of the Tabard Inn in George Street is occupied by a different type of facility! In the background, along Spicer Street, is the Abbey School.

THE TUDOR TAVERN 2004 S2705k (Tom Doig)

The former George Inn and Swan Inn (subsequently called the King's Head) were combined in the 1960s to form the picturesque Tudor Tavern in George Street.

Between Romeland Hill and the old gateway to the Abbey lies Romeland Garden. It was here that George Tankerfield, a Yorkshire cook, was burned at the stake on 26th August 1555 for being a Protestant. On the night before his martyrdom, whilst lodging at the Chequers Inn, he had the fire built up and placed his leg in the flames to assure himself that he was able to withstand the pain and avoid jeopardising his faith by crying for mercy.

W T Phillips wrote about Tankerfield's execution place in Romeland:

Come, see where he lay, 'tis a quiet green space,
George Tankerfield, martyr, was burnt in this place,
Behold where poor Tankerfield lay!
The graves of the dead have since hallow'd that plot,
The leaves of yon willow may point to the spot
Where he smouldered in ashes away.

To the south of Romeland Garden is the Abbey's 14th-century great monastery Gateway, once the prison and later St Albans School. The original Gateway was blown down in a gale on 15th January 1362 and the present Gateway was built for Abbot de la Mere c1365 as part of the later fortifying wall. A plaque on the Gate tells us that 'it was besieged by the Insurgents during the Peasant Revolt, 1381. Made Liberty Prison 1553. Sessions held here till 1651. Occupied by French soldiers in the Napoleonic Wars.' Many of the 'Insurgents' paid the ultimate price and were beheaded here. It is thought that their heads may have been displayed on the ramparts. Here, in 1479 following those of Caxton and his assistant, Wynkyn de Worde at Westminster and Oxford, the third printing press in England was built for a 'sometyme scole mayster of Seynt Albans.' It is believed that the press was located in a second floor room containing a fire place and later with the arms of Charles I on the wall. For many years it was known as the

King Charles Room - it was later furnished as the school memorial library. Amongst the printed editions of several important books was the 'Boke of St Albans,' a treatise on hunting and the blazoning of arms in part colour ascribed by some to the semi-mythical Dame Juliana Berners, Prioress of Sopwell. The middle portion on hunting is in verse and contains the words: 'Explice Dam Juliana Barnes in her boke of huntyng.' It is a fine piece of work and the chapters on fishing excel even Isaac Walton's work.

GEORGE TANKERFIELD TESTS HIS CONVICTION
ZZZ01719 (From 'Nonconformity in Hertfordshire by Urwick 1884)

The evening before his execution by burning at the stake, George Tankerfield tested himself by placing his leg in an open fire. He wanted to make sure he would not cry out in public.

ENGRAVING OF THE KING CHARLES ROOM, ST ALBANS GATEWAY ZZZ01718

It is believed that this is the room in which the third press in England printed 'The Boke of St Albans'.

At the foot of Abbey Mill Lane, overlooking the River Ver, is the Fighting Cocks Inn, sometimes in the past known as the Round House. It stands on an embankment at the edge of what was the king's fishpool. The cellar is constructed of stone blocks which appear to have come from the monastic buildings. As the inn stands only a few feet above the level of the river, the foundations have been carefully laid to prevent excessive dampness entering the cellar. The walls and floor are built from compounded flints and the lower walls are carefully bonded with more flints and Roman tiles.

The Clock Tower

Dominating the site of the Market Cross is the Clock Tower. The people of St Albans were devastated by the failure of the Peasant's Revolt in 1381 and, as Tony Billings says, the Tower is thought to have been erected between 1403 and 1412 to 'cock a snook at the Abbey.' Indeed, there were rumours that the Lollards intended to destroy the Abbey if the opportunity arose. Outside the jurisdiction of the Abbey, the 77 feet high Clock Tower was built of brick, stone and infilled flint and served to hold the curfew bell. No record exists of the source of the bell but there is no doubt that it was cast in 1335 and is inscribed 'Missi de coelis habeo nomen Gabrielis' - 'I carry the heaven-sent name of Gabriel.' Gabriel rang for royal deaths, fires, casualties or affray and to tell the apprentices to be prepared to start work. It is also said that it rang the alarm when the Yorkists launched a surprise attack on St Albans during the Wars of the Roses. The first mention of

a clock appears in 1485 when one Robert Grane was granted a lease starting at the 'Feest of Seynt Michell thark Aungell' in exchange for which he was to 'kepe, make and rewle the clokke.' A second bell, cast in 1729 and moved from the Market House (demolished in 1855) was rung at 4am and 8pm to indicate the start and finish of trading in the market. The clock on the Tower strikes the hours. Around the base, a group of traders shacks had been erected whilst the ground floor was leased as a shop. By 1700, the tower was in a poor structural state and plans were tabled to demolish it but it was reprieved, restored and sold. For a short while the Clock Tower operated as the town's post office and a few years later, during the Napoleanic Wars, a 20 feet high timber, shuttered frame was mounted on the roof. This was part of the telegraph system and was used as one of the stages sending Admiralty messages from Dover to London and from London

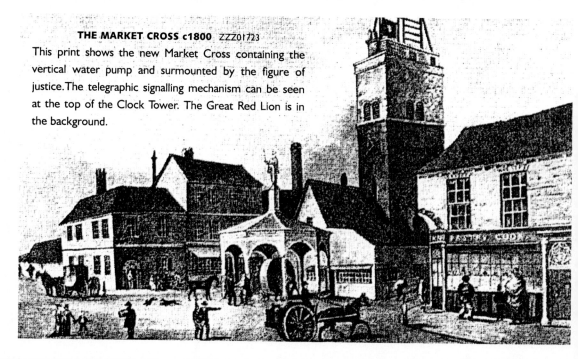

THE MARKET CROSS c1800 ZZZ01723
This print shows the new Market Cross containing the vertical water pump and surmounted by the figure of justice. The telegraphic signalling mechanism can be seen at the top of the Clock Tower. The Great Red Lion is in the background.

to Great Yarmouth and Liverpool. When Napoleon was defeated in 1814, the shutters were removed but the signallers' hut remained in place for another forty years.

The Clock Tower underwent further restoration in 1865, under the direction of Gilbert Scott, at a expenditure of £800 when it cost the people an extra 2d rate to pay the £152 for the clock to be 'illuminated automatically at night by incandescent gas.' Further work was subsequently carried out when, after clearing away the lean-to sheds, the area in front was cobbled making it a popular meeting place for visitors and towns people alike. The Tower is open to the public at week-ends and bank holidays. Climbing the 97 steps takes the visitor past Gabriel and through the five internal stories to the roof where there is a unique and almost uninterrupted view of the City and the cathedral.

THE CLOCK TOWER c1830 ZZZ01716
The Market Cross after the removal of the Telegraph System and the demolition of the ocatgonal pump house.

It is possible that the building was at the base of a corner turret to the wall that surrounded the monastery but this is unlikely. A much better candidate is the converted dovecote, for a document dated 1622 in the Public Record Office at Kew tell us that at St 'Albones', 'Thomas Preston bought an Olde Pigeon House and pulled the same downe and erected it ... and afterwards put up a chimney and made thereof a tenement which is now called the Rounde House.' The possibility is reinforced by evidence from the time of Abbot Moote (1396-1401) who had in his garden a 'skilfully made pigeon house' which would have had a roof identical to that of the Fighting Cocks. The monastery was demolished in 1539 and it may be that this was the building bought by Thomas Preston and re-erected around 1609 on the site of St Germain's Gate on the embankment by the Ver.

The Fighting Cocks is steeped in tradition and mystery. It is said that Oliver Cromwell spent the night here and stabled his horse in the small half-timbered room. Why he would want to do this when one of the few buildings to survive the demolition of the monastery was the stable block is confusing! Another says that the pub was used as a meeting place for cock-fighters. However, no evidence has ever been found and the room would have been too small to hold the cock-pit, spectators and betting 'johnnies.' Of course, it may have been a place for private challenges but was hardly the main cock-fighting centre in the town. After cock-fighting was made illegal, the beerhouse changed its name to the Fisherman. It finally achieved a full licence as late as 1951! During the early 1970s, the Fighting Cocks was totally and sympathetically restored by the brewers Ind Coope.

The Almshouses in Hatfield Road were built, under an indenture of 2nd June 1736, to provide accommodation for widows and maiden daughters of military officers but this was soon changed to 18 men and 18 women who lived 'soberly and piously.' A cartouche bearing the arms of the Marlborough family remind us that the benefactress was Sarah, widow of John Churchill, Duke of Marlborough.

Sarah had made her fortune of over £100,000 by selling her shares just before the bursting of the South Sea Bubble. She and her husband lived in Holywell House and entertained many members of the nobility including the future Queen Anne. This was not the present Holywell House – Sarah's house stood at the bottom of Holywell Hill and was demolished in 1837.

THE FIGHTING COCKS 1921 70484p

In 1622 Thomas Preston bought 'an old Pigeon House and re-erected it' near the Silk Mill. It became the Fighting Cocks public house, a favourite weekend meeting place offering good beer.

HATFIELD ROAD ALMSHOUSES 2004
S2715k (Tom Doig)

Founded in 1736, these almshouses were originally built for the widows and daughters of military officers, but soon afterwards were opened to 18 men and 18 women who lived 'soberly and piously'.

The White Hart Inn has a long and interesting history. In 1746 Hogarth painted a portrait of the 80 year old Simon Fraser, Lord Lovat when he stopped at the White Hart, on Holywell Hill, on his way to the Tower of London to be executed for his part in the '45 Rebellion of Prince Charles Edward Stewart. Engraved copies of the portrait sold like hot cakes but the original portrait was lost. The portrait, found, it is said, about 80 years later 'in the house of a poor person in the neighbourhood of St Albans,' now hangs in the National Portrait Gallery (although there is a fine copy in the White Hart.) It shows a remarkably cheerful person for one who was to die very soon.

HOLYWELL HILL c1921 70480p

The Fleur de Lys was built around 1430 and then substantially rebuilt in the 16th and 17th centuries around a cobbled courtyard. In the 18th century it was extended further back over what is now Verulam Road. The yard contained granaries, stables, hay-lofts, coach-houses and a bowling green. It rented out saddle horses and single-horse post chaises - the two seater sports cars of the 18th century. In the early 1800s, a fire broke out in the stables and caused a great deal of damage to the nearby cottages. John Richardson, who regularly brought his renowned travelling theatre to St Albans for the Michelmas Fair, contributed the takings, amounting to just over £100, from the performances. His theatre was held in a huge tent, over 100 feet long and thirty feet wide, and was hung with green baize and red plush draperies. There was seating for an audience of 1000.

Did you know?

There was a Blue Coat charity school, founded in 1713, in Fishpool Street. By 1857, its finances were in a a 'very depressed state' and the town clerk of the Corporation was instructed to write to the vicars of the parishes of St Michael and the adjacent St Peter with a view to them arranging an annual collection to support the school. It is not recorded how successful this was but eventually, the Blue Coat School merged with St Alban's Anglican National School.

Hogarth had met his friend, Dr Joshua Webster at the White Hart. Webster had a practise in the town and spent his spare time writing on antiquarian subjects. Of St Albans, he recorded, 'The town of St Albans is situated upon rising ground and capable as being laid as dry and clean as any town in the kingdom, but by bad management is a very dirty one in winter.' Webster and Hogarth were known to Dr Nathaniel Cotton who cared for the mentally ill and owned a private asylum, the 'Collegium Insanorum' in St Peter's Street, where William Cowper was treated during his bouts of mental illness. Cowper had applied for a post of clerk in the House of Lords but the prospect of the examination and interview turned his mind and he attempted suicide. He was admitted to the Insanorum and took to evangelical Christianity. Eventually he discharged himself, noting in his journal of 7th June 1765, 'Having spent eighteen months in St Albans, partly in bondage, I took my leave at 4 in the morning, and set out for Cambridge.'

In August 1793, Thomas Robinson, who had been a waiter at the White Hart for 40 years, died. The 'Gentleman's Magazine' reported, 'by his attention and acquaintance with the antiquities of the place he rendered himself useful to all guests.' He was, clearly, someone that this writer on St Albans wished he had met. The 'Gentleman's Magazine' had also reported, in 1770, on the divorce proceedings of Lord Grosvenor against his pretty wife who was found guilty of 'criminal conversation' at the White Hart with the Duke of Cumberland, brother of King George III.

At the lower end of Holywell Hill, Sopwell Lane led to the Nunnery of Sopwell. Like the White Hart, legends say that it was the marriage place of Henry VIII and Anne Boleyn. It was demolished at the dissolution of the monasteries in 1539 and a few years later a mansion was built on the site by Sir Richard Lee. Very little of either remains today.

SOPWELL NUNNERY 1921 70482

Although known as Sopwell Nunnery, these are the ruins of a house built by Sir Richard Lee in the 1500s after the dissolution of the monasteries.

Until the building, in 1826, of Thomas Telford's new Verulam Road as part of his Holyhead Road, Fishpool Street was the main road leading westwards out of the city and, it is said, 72 coaches each day thundered along its length. It took its name from the great fishpool that lay along its southern boundary and runs from the bottom of Romeland Hill to Kingsbury Mill. In earlier times, Romeland Hill was known as Hockerhulle whilst the lower part, close to the Mill, was called the Sally Path (or Salipath). This appropriate name probably derives from its position at the extremity of the town where people could 'sally forth' on their journeys. The architecture of Fishpool Street remains almost intact as a testimony to the far-sighted Surveyor to the Council, Albert Moody, who was instrumental in ensuring the survival and 'listing' of many of its unique buildings.

Shops and inns occupied the main part of the south side of George Street. Many of these inns would have provided a welcome short rest for travellers and to give the ostlers and grooms the opportunity to change the horses. A single team of horses did not pull the coaches all the way from London but rather they changed the horses at each 'stage' - hence the name 'stage coaches.' The horses just shuttled back and forth between two stage stops and always ended up in their own stable stall at the end of their shift. The stall would carry a painted plate bearing the name of the horse - Captain, Star, Satan, Blackie, etc. The grooms were very proud of the condition of their animals and the stalls, working long hours to clean and polish the harness and its decorations.

Usually a stage would be about 15 miles but, in the case of St Albans, each stage ended with a long haul up a hill and therefore the stages may have been a little shorter. In 1797, the Holyhead coach took an hour and a half to cover the 12 miles from London to Barnet where the first change of horses took place; another hour and a half for the 11 miles to St Albans for the second change and then a long, leisurely, almost walking pace, journey of thirty and a half miles to Lathbury taking about four and a half hours. The coach left London at eight o'clock in the evening pulling into Mr Swetman's inn (unfortunately not named) at St Albans in time for a snack at eleven. The courtyard would have been lit by flaming torches carried by the 'link men' who solicited rewards from the passengers as they guided them across the slippery and steaming cobbles onto the duck-boarding and through

to the privvies and, later, the warming drinks and snacks. Then it would be on to Northamptonshire. The coach arrived at Holyhead at five o'clock in the morning two days later having taken forty-four and half hours to cover the 279 miles. After Telford's improvements to the road, the time was reduced to twenty seven hours. Interestingly, Thomas Swetman (or Sweetman) had been a Guard on the Chester Mail. In January 1795, the leather traces on his coach snapped as they were passing through the southern outskirts of Chester and he was forced to wade through water up to his hips and repair the broken leather. He was badly frost-bitten and had to retire. Thomas Hasker, Superintendent of Mail-Coaches, solicited a pension of 10s per week from the Postmaster General. This was enough for him to buy the inn at St Albans in 1796.

An indication of the weight of traffic in the area can be gained from a description written by Solomon George Shaw, bookseller and stationer, who lived in the town in 1813:

'The mails and stage coaches which run through the town (supposing them to be pretty well loaded) have accommodation for upward of six hundred passengers daily: add to which the number of travellers who pass through in other conveyances and those on foot, it may reasonably be computed that not less than 1000 persons pass through the town every day.'

The inns had large courtyards to turn the coaches which were surrounded by stalls and fodder stores with, above them, galleries containing withdrawing and eating-rooms. Surprisingly large numbers of 'stage horses' were kept. One so-called 'coaching inn' in the north east of Hertfordshire, on the London to Kings Lynn route, records that it retained 96 horses and a reliable source suggests that at one time 1400 horses were stabled in St Albans. Rather like the Formula 1 car racing engineers, the ostlers vied with each other as to who could change a team of horses fastest - a time of under four minutes was not unusual. This was not enough time for many passengers who had been looking forward to a 'comfort-break' after a liquid lunch and a bumpy ride up Fishpool Street or Holywell Hill! The entrance to the courtyards were usually just wide enough for one coach and a system of signalling was needed to avoid blocking the archway. A railway-type signal was often mounted just at the top of the arch - a long arm said do not enter whilst a short arm indicated that all was clear. Indeed, there is still a public house at Lemsford, close to St Albans, known as the Long and Short Arm.

With coaches turning and blocking the road waiting for their chance to enter or leave the inns there was much confusion and the occasional collision at the junction. In 1812, George Street had to be widened to provide clearance for the coaches travelling from London through St Albans to Chester and on to Holyhead.

By the late 1700s, it became clear that the arrangement for traffic along Old London Road and up Holywell Hill and left into the High Street for Fishpool Street was causing unacceptable congestion and delay. The combination of the normal road traffic, the 72 or so stage coaches each day (as listed later in 1826) and the market traders meant that a drastic solution was needed. This solution was to drive a new road from the toll gate up the hill to emerge at Chequer Street (then called Halliwell Street) opposite the High Street and just north of the Peahen Hotel. To ensure a gradual and even rise, part of the new road had to be raised as much as twelve feet above the original ground level. Many of the shops, houses and Melbourn-Cooper's cinema, whether on the north or south side of London Road, were built on platform terraces and had steep slopes at their rear.

One consequence of bringing the 'new' London Road into the middle of the town was the need for the demolition of the Cross Keys (sometimes the Peter Keys) Inn; another was the closure of many of the coaching inns at the top of Holywell Hill and Sopwell Lane. A new Cross Keys was built on the corner of London Road and Chequer Street and provided a hire service for open and closed carriages. In time, the new road led to congestion at the cross roads and in 1938, traffic lights were installed to control the flow of vehicles.

SOPWELL NUNNERY 1921 70482

HIGH STREET 1921 70476p

The High Street is seen here with the Great Red Lion in the background. The Great Red Lion Hotel, at the corner of the High Street, was built on the site of an old coaching inn. It was said to have had an underground stable from which ran a subterranean passage leading to the Abbey. Originally known as Cornerhall in the 13th century, it had become the Lion by the 16th century. In 1792 it was refronted and renamed the Great Red Lion to distinguish it from the other Red Lions in St Albans. It was rebuilt in 1896 and finally closed in 1981 after which it became a shop.

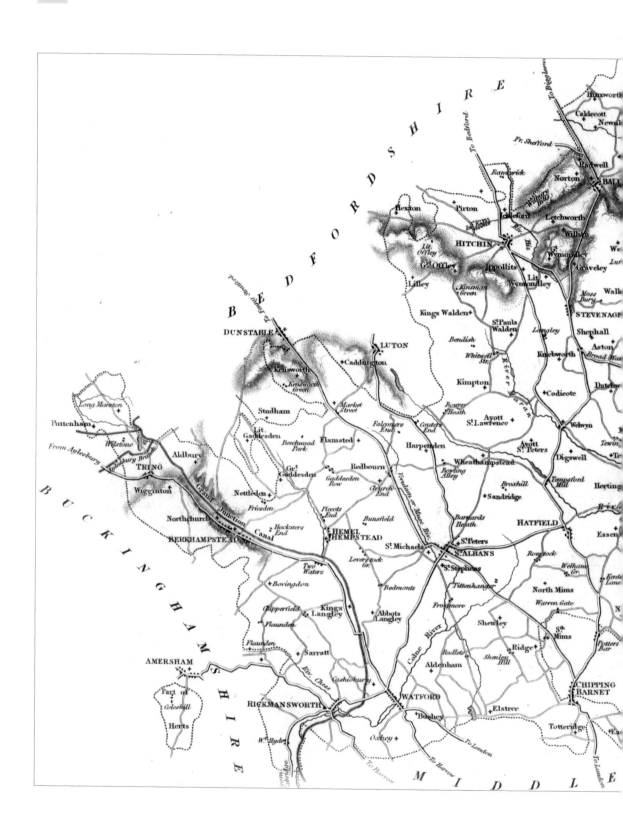

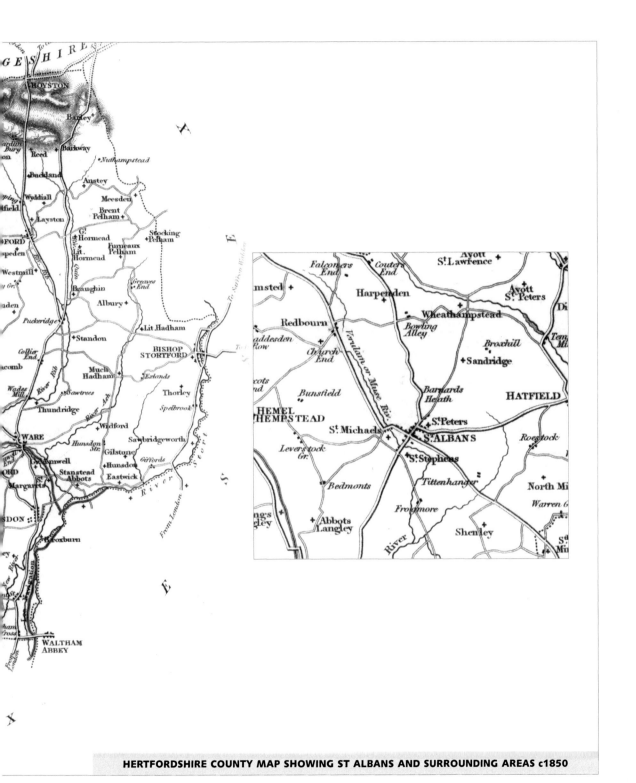

HERTFORDSHIRE COUNTY MAP SHOWING ST ALBANS AND SURROUNDING AREAS c1850

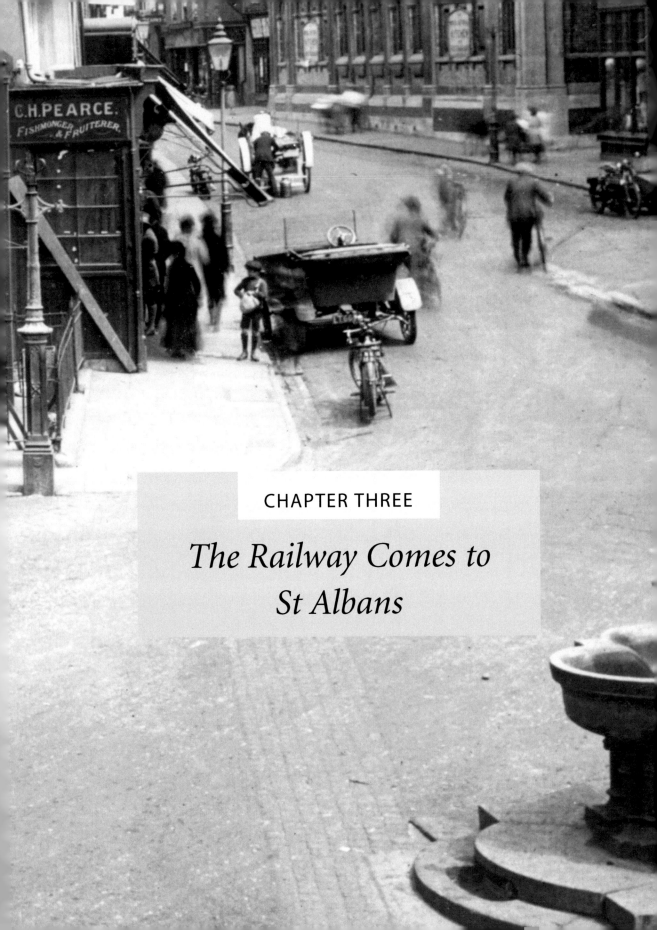

CHAPTER THREE

*The Railway Comes to
St Albans*

AT THE junction of Victoria Street and Marlborough Road, three of the four corners were occupied by straw hat making factories in the 19th century. Nigel Goose in his analysis of the 1851 census for St Albans (University of Hertfordshire, 2000) tells us that over 1350 people were directly involved in the manufacturing of straw hats in the town.

Many of these were young girls between the ages of 10 and 14 years. Some plaiters had made up their own hats although most sold their lengths of plait through factors to the hat makers at Luton. Plaiting wheat straw into strips to be made up into bonnets and hats had been a country craft for many years but, towards the middle of the 19th century, St Albans was home to a number of straw hat factories. George Shaw, writing in 1812, says, 'The straw plat (sic) sewing is a source of employment for many females in the town from which they may derive, and also from platting the straws, a respectable and comfortable livelihood.' He goes on to say that St Albans' straw-plait market was 'one of the largest in England which begins at the ringing of a bell by one of the beadles of the borough and terminates before the commencement of the corn market.' The straw-plait market took place through Waxhouse Gate in School Lane. In 1858, when a celebratory parade took place after the opening of St Albans' first railway station, one of the most talked about displays was of a 'chaste white Leghorn plait [bonnet] of delicate texture and of elegant sloping shape - henceforth to be styled in the trade [as] The St Albans Railway Opening.' Another style

was called The St Albans First Class Carriage! Among the major straw hat manufacturers in the town were William Westell, and Henry Partridge Smith, whose factory was one of those at the cross-roads.

Some of the houses in Fishpool Street have interesting and unusual features. One house has false windows. The two windows above the front door are not real - the apertures in the brickwork are correctly built and the frames painted white but there is no glass, just the black shapes painted on rendered cement. This was possibly to avoid paying the Window Tax but was more likely an attempt to maintain the architectural balance.

FISHPOOL STREET 2004 S2703k (Tom Doig)

In the 18th and 19th centuries, with the buildings built cheek by jowl, they were particularly susceptible to fire. Insurance was an expensive investment and few families were able to afford the premiums. Houses which were covered and could expect help from the retained fire brigade carried a lead or brass 'fire mark' high up on a front wall. Few survive but one fine example is to be seen above the door of 92 Fishpool Street telling us, and the firemen, that we would be paid by the insurance company for saving the building and contents should it catch fire. Throughout St Albans, there are some similar fire marks and it is clear that during its short life (1824-1831), the Hertfordshire, Cambridgeshire and County Fire Office provided cover for many of the premises in the town.

To the north of the eastern end of Fishpool Street stands what had been the open space of Romeland where the town's weekly and three annual fairs were held. In the medieval period, Roomland, as it was then called, would have seen the bustle and chaos of market stalls and booths.

By the late 1600s, buildings began to encroach onto 'the void place of ground called Romeland' and the fair was moved elsewhere. In 1825, when the town council was looking to replace the inadequate old Town Hall, Romeland was suggested as a possible site but the idea was rejected. The remains of Romeland were bought by the Corporation for £120 in 1839 and it was proposed, in 1855, to use the locality for a railway terminal on the line to Watford. After the intervention of the Earl of Verulam, the project came to nothing and house building continued.

Facing onto Romeland Gardens, Romeland House was built for Frederick Vandermeulen by Sir Christopher Wrens's master mason. Standing on the Gardens was a row of five blue-doored dwellings known as Blue Row. When they were demolished in 1823, the timber and fittings were sold for £171. Some records suggest that Romeland is a corruption of 'roome-land' - a meeting ground. This is an appropriate name for a place where all sorts of people, dead or alive, meet. It had been the site of one of two Abbey charnel houses - collecting rooms for displaced bones; a burial ground - where the monks of the Abbey gathered for the last time, and today is a secluded garden where office and shopworkers meet for a quiet lunch. They can sit surrounded by ancient gravestones and by a huge block of untouched grey granite engraved in a Roman typeface with the words, 'Vota, Vita, Mea' - 'My life is devoted.'

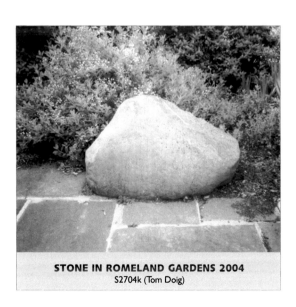

STONE IN ROMELAND GARDENS 2004
S2704k (Tom Doig)

The Abbey Gateway makes a fine goal mouth for these young
footballers. However, they would have been shooed away by
the monks to make way for stately religious processions 500
years before.

THE ABBEY GATEWAY c1955 S2096

The Gateway survived the Abbey's dissolution in 1538 and is the sole surviving out-building. Later, until 1866 it was used firstly as the Abbot's prison and then as the town gaol. In 1851, the underground accommodation held 43 inmates, including two women, overseen by the Prison Governor and the Head Turnkey. In April 1860, the town watch committee presented a report condemning the conditions in the cells. A prisoner had died and the inquest recorded that the cause was the state of the prison. It was proposed that the lower rooms of the Clock Tower should be converted into a police station and that a new block of cells should be built butting against the base of the Tower. The proposal came to nothing. When the new St Albans prison at Grimston Road just beyond the main line railway station was built in 1867, the Trustees of the Grammar School took over the building and moved the pupils here from the Lady Chapel in 1871 where it continued to be used as the main school until 1908. The School had been founded around 950 and was operated under the rule of the Abbott. Today it houses the School Library for the 800 or so pupils.

THE CORN EXCHANGE 2004 S2719k (Tom Doig)

The Corn Exchange was opened in September 1857 with a great dinner with toasts and speeches. Today it has been turned into shops, and customers can leave their cycles in the penny-farthing bicycle racks in the left foreground.

In the mid to late 1800s, a tallow factory stood at the junction of Verulam Road and George Street. The smell was appalling and in 1875 a petition was raised and presented to the Council, 'The stench arising from the tallow fat and other ingredients is most offensive and intolerable to the surrounding neighbourhood .... we trust that you will adopt such measures as may be necessary to abate the nuisance.' The owner was Edward Sutton Wiles, the once and future Mayor of St Albans - he was allowed to get away with the 'nuisance' for another ten years but eventually he moved the factory to Bernard's Heath, off the Harpenden Road, where, it is said, it continued it's smelly activities. Incidentally, Bernard's Heath, the site of one of the town's brickworks, is mentioned in Dickens' Bleak House'.

The Market Place is dominated by the Corn Exchange (now shops). This was opened at a grand dinner on 23rd September 1857. The elected members of the Town Council imposed their own restrictions on its use and the townspeople revolted causing a small riot in December 1859. When the Councillors did not step down, the farmers, corn-dealers and traders decided to boycott the Corn Exchange and faced with a massive loss in revenue, on the 26th December 1860, the Councillors gave way. The following February, as James Corbett tells us, 'the farmers .. returned victorious to their Corn Exchange.'

During the 18th and early 19th century, bribery and corruption was rife during parliamentary elections. In 1851, prior to the election contest between Mr Jacob Bell and Alderman Carden, the situation was so bad and the corruption so open that a parliamentary investigation was mounted. It appeared that votes could be bought on the open market and, indeed, Sovereign Alley which runs between the Market Place and Chequer Street was a recognised meeting place where payment of a sovereign would ensure that your poll would increase by at least one. It's reputation ensured that, from that day, the name Sovereign Alley (or Lane as the later city fathers preferred) still survives today.

SOVEREIGN ALLEY 2004 S2720k (Tom Doig)

During the parliamentary elections of 1851 the payment of a sovereign would buy a vote. The agents of corrupt candidates would meet their clients in Sovereign Alley.

MARKET PLACE c1950 S2075t

Another case was the subtle bribe of £88 13s paid to John 'Thomas' Blanks, landlord of the White Hart and hat trimming maker, for services rendered in driving one journey to London and providing a few meals. The Parliamentary Commission set up to investigate was not impressed and the town was, for 35 years, deprived of the two parliamentary representatives.

At the southern end of the Market Place, where it meets the High Street, is the original site of Mrs Worley's fountain. Mrs Isabella Worley (1817-1883), sister of Arthur Timperton of Childwick Hall and a wealthy widow, who lived at Sopwell House, gave this ornamental fountain to the town in 1872. The fountain was designed by Mr (later Sir) George Gilbert Scott who was working on the Tower and in the process of preparing a report on the condition of the Abbey. The bowl weighed 3 tons and was turned from Mull granite and the centre crocket finial from yellow

MARKET CROSS 1921 70477xp

Mrs Isabella Worley of Sopwell House gave this fountain to the town in 1872. The owner of the open car parked outside C H Pearce, fishmonger and fruiterer, has a long wait if he thinks he will soon be able to buy some spares. Although the shop would soon become Halfords, they started out selling only bicycle spares.

Mansfield Wodehouse stone with a Devonshire marble moulding. The columns supporting the bowl are cylinders of Peterhead granite. Four bronze animal heads spout the water into the bowl which overflows into a trough for dogs and there was an additional step for the children. The fountain was manufactured by Farmer & Brindley of Lambeth at a total cost of £500. Mrs Worley was a well known benefactor to the town providing clothing and meat each Christmas to the poor children and supporting various orphanages and hospitals. The town council and Scott had wanted the new fountain to be placed in St Peter's Street but Mrs Worley was adamant that it was being built 'for the greater good of the poor' and that the final site was the only option. Mrs Worley was not present when her fountain was unveiled on 10th June 1872.

The fountain was moved again in 1883 to the site proposed by Scott. This to-ing and fro-ing prompted one councillor, William Hurlock, to suggest that the fountain should be placed on wheels so that it could be moved without expense when members changed their minds. It stood in front of the Clock Tower for many years until the 1920s when it was removed as it was becoming an obstruction to traffic. It returned when the area was pedestrianised but was moved to the courtyard of Victoria Square, Grimston Road on the site of the old gaol in 1993.

When the fountain was removed in the 1920s, the centre ended up in a garden in St Peter's Street and the top part in Lord Brocket's garden in London Road. The bottom piece was later displayed as a feature in Thrale's restaurant. They gave it to the Council in 1964 who managed to obtain the section held by Lord Brocket. The parts were brought together and the complete and restored fountain now stands in Victoria Square.

The market area in front of the Town Hall experienced many public meetings; some quiet and restrained whilst others were good-humoured and noisy.

The public announcement by Mr Edwards, the town clerk, of the Royal Charter, dated 28th August 1877, raising St Albans from a town to a city was made here on 13th September. At every mention of the word city the crowd whooped and yelled and threw their hats into the air. The Abbey was elevated to a Cathedral although everyone continued to call it The Abbey and a new Bishop, Thomas Claughton, was enthroned on 12th June.

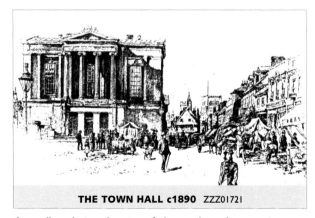

THE TOWN HALL c1890 ZZZ01721

As well as being the site of the market, the area in front of the Town Hall saw meetings, rallies and public proclamations. When the Royal Charter was granted to St Albans in 1877, the announcement that it was to become a city was made here.

MARKET PLACE 1921 70475p

For the three centuries after the dissolution the condition of the Abbey declined and one by one the out-buildings were dismantled as a source of building materials. By the start of the 1800s it was clear that either the Abbey (and parish church to
St Albans) would have to be demolished or totally restored. Work commenced in the 1850s shoring up the walls and facades with timber baulks but the cost of complete renovations was soon found to be beyond the pocket of St Albans. On 31st July 1871, cracks appeared in the tower pillars. It appeared that the pillars had been hollowed out and shored with timber in preparation for firing. This would have demolished the tower and was, therefore, thought to have been prepared shortly after the dissolution. Fortunately the project came to naught and the tower survived. The work commenced on the Abbey but the town was unable to provide the expensive budget. The £50,000 project had been entrusted to Sir Gilbert Scott but he died shortly after the start of the work. Lord Grimthorpe stepped in and offered to underwrite the cost of the restoration of what was now the cathedral on condition that his design was accepted. Although there were minor grumblings, it was agreed and the restoration was completed.

Today, harsh words have been said about Grimthorpe's interpretation of a cathedral but there is no doubt that, without his influence, the great building would have been lost and, in all probability, its site would now be office blocks and shopping centres. The Abbey continues to expand and develop. A new chapter house, adjoining the south transept, was added in 1982 and opened by the Queen.

THE ABBEY, THE WEST FRONT 1921 70457

There has been some criticism of Grimthorp's interpretation of a medieval cathedral but this view shows that it has stood the test of time.

In 1881, Henry Jenkin Gotto, an Oxford Street, London, stationer, arranged to have rows of lime trees planted on either side of St Peter's Street. A few years later, in 1906, the people of the town arose with one voice. Modern technology was about to destroy the attractive view along the street. James Corbett in his History of St Albans tells us that what aroused their anger was the Postmaster-General's decision that telegraph poles would have to be erected along the west side; no other option was available. The lines had to be above ground; underground wires were unsuitable for technical reasons. The only concession would be that the pole, usually of wood, could be of ornamental cast iron. Letters were written, petitions raised and a public protest meeting took place at the Corn Exchange. Eventually the PMG gave way under 'the force of public pressure' and, as James Corbett says, 'To this day there are no telephone poles in St Peter's Street.'

St Peter's Church

St Peter's Church is one of three reputed to have been founded around 948 by Abbot Ulsinus (sometimes Wulsin). Before 1400, it was in the very heart of a parish of more than 20 square miles, and, as David Dean noted, 'up to the reign of Elizabeth I accommodated most of the town's burials.' It was among the gravestones of these deceased that, much to the annoyance of the parishioners, cattle roamed and pulled the grass. In 1787, the local people complained to the vicar. The tower of St Peter's was partly demolished in 1799 and the internal bell ringing room floor collapsed in 1801. The following year, the tower was rebuilt and rendered with cement and the transepts removed. By the end of the 1800s, the condition of the church was causing concern and Lord Grimthorp underwrote the cost of its restoration which left very few of the 15th century features intact. The work was completed in 1908. At the end of the Second World War, a victory peal of 5056 changes, known as Bob Major, was rung in three hours and nine minutes. A window in the bell chamber of the church commemorates this feat by members of the Hertford County Association of Change Ringers (St Peter's Society) of 16th August 1945.

ST PETER'S CHURCH 2004 S2711k (Tom Doig)

The railway under Victoria Street came to St Albans in 1868. The LNWR to Watford was opened at the Abbey Station in May 1858 whilst the Great Northern line linked with the Abbey and London Road Stations in October 1865, but it was the opening of what came to be known as City Station in October 1868 for the Midland railway that truly connected St Albans to London to the south and Bedford to the north. When the station was built, a canopy was erected at the entrance so that the town's dignitaries could alight from their coaches directly into the station and avoid becoming drenched in wet weather. Indeed, early photographs show the awning with a carriage parked adjacent to it.

The need for a railway link between London and St Albans was recognised as early as the 1840s and on 5th May 1858, after the building of Abbey Station, the first train from Watford, bedecked with flags and evergreens, steamed into the town, and there was a great celebration with parades and feasting. Ninety railway navvies in white smocks with pink and white ribbons in their caps led the processions. They were followed by the St Albans brass band in new crimson caps and huge gold tassles. Then came the display by the straw plaiters workers from the town's factories, each group marching under its own company banner. The boys from the Blue Coat School came next followed by the borough police in their new uniforms. The mayor in his official robe of scarlet and ermine was accompanied by the beadle, mace-bearer, aldermen and town councillors. At the Assembly Rooms, a cold collation

Did you know?

It was intended that Clarence Park would be opened by the Duke of Clarence, known affectionately as 'Eddy' and once thought to be a possible candidate for Jack the Ripper, but he died in January 1892 so the ceremony was conducted by George, Duke of Cambridge.

Did you know?

Close to the junction of Hatfield Road and St Peter's Street stood the town's stray animal

dinner was provided by Thomas Blanks of the White Hart. This was the same Thomas Blanks who had been bribed to the tune of £88 13s during the election scandal of 1851. Blanks, with his wife, Eliza, and their children, had only arrived in St Albans from Rochford in Essex in 1850 but appears to have made an immediate impact by throwing himself into the life of the town. A long list of toasts to 'the town and trade of St Albans' was then proposed and seconded, interspersed with songs and speeches. Later, in the meadow opposite the station, there was a programme of sports and amusements including foot, pony and donkey races. All the children were presented with a bun! The day ended with a ball in the Corn Exchange when the music was provided by a Quadrille

Band. It is possible that the refined pupils and students who attended Eliza Upton's school for 6 to 16 year old young ladies from their home at 8, London Road may have heard the sound of jollification for, a week or so later, a letter was received from her husband, the Rev William Upton, a local non-conformist minister: 'Are the authorities not aware that dancing rooms are degrading and demoralizing? I was not present personally at the public dinner, but am informed that it was by no means worthy of this town.' As for the field sports, this spoilsport says that they were the scene of 'disgusting intemperance, injured health, lost character, expulsions from situations previously held, corruption of public morals, contraction of fearful guilt.'

Maybe the town worthies took notice for there is no record of any festivities when the Hatfield and St Albans line was opened in 1865 and only a few flags at the opening of the City Station in 1868.

It would be only fair to mention here that this was not the first time that St Albans experienced steam powered travel. A steam powered coach, operated by the London and St Albans Steam Carriage Company, had run through the town in the period around 1835 taking passengers from London to Birmingham. It reached the unheard of speed of 25 miles per hour and carried fifty passengers but swingeing toll charges doomed this innovation to failure. The toll gates, in turn, fell to the onslaught of the railways for they were closed in 1871 when it became clear that the cost of their maintenance far outstripped the revenue.

SKETCH OF A STEAM COACH ZZZ01724

Neither the railway station at the bottom of Victoria Street, nor its predecessor at the Abbey, was the first form of steam transport to come to St Albans. There had been a steam coach which, it is claimed, reached a speed of 25mph. It failed when the Red Flag Act was imposed that required any horseless carriage should be preceded by a man on foot carrying a red flag!

The arrival of the railways sounded the death knell of the coaching trade. Some coaches were still in operation until 1868 and 'The Wonder' ran occasional summer services to London until 1893. One or two of the town's carters continued to take hay to London (the capital needed a constant supply of fodder for its many horse drawn vans, cabs, drays, etc) and brought back animal (and human!) manure for fertilisation. Manure of any type was a precious commodity. 'Night soil' from the privies of London was in great demand on the chalky land and dog manure, called 'pure' was exported from St Albans to the tanneries in the east end of the capital.

The town's gas works, which had been built in 1826, were located close to Abbey Station for ease of delivery of coal and coke. Two of the original four 1903 gas holders survive at the end of Leyland Avenue. Tony Billings tells us that the concrete coke producing retort was demolished in 1975. With the arrival of North Sea gas, the remainder of the site was razed and redeveloped into shops and offices.

Of course, steam did not last forever and the diesel service was introduced in the City Station in the early 1960s. The number of trains increased to over 100 per week and the journey time to London was reduced to less that half an hour. Then, 1983, it was the turn of an electric service which reduced the time to 20 minutes and provided a direct service to Gatwick and the south coast.

Over the railway bridge at the bottom of Victoria Street, facing onto Grimston Road, is the City Gaol. Originally, the Borough and Liberty prisoners had been held in the Abbey Gatehouse, in the cells in the Town Hall in Dagnal Street or from 1831 under the Town Hall in the Market Place. The new prison, erected in 1866/7, contained a tread mill, worked by the prisoners, which pumped water for the town. Until 1874 it was used only for criminals from the local area but because of the need for additional accommodation due to restricted space at Hertford, it was designated a prison for the whole county. A few years later, in 1878, Hertford prison was closed and the convicts transferred to St Albans. It not only had accommodation for 99 convicted criminals but saw a number of executions. One hanging was that of Mary Ansell in July 1899. Up to the last, she protested that she had not poisoned her sister for the £10 insurance money. Despite appeals to the Home Office and Queen Victoria, the

sentence was carried out. It is said that, on his death bed, her brother confessed to the crime. The final execution took place and the last black flag was flown in 1914; the gaol was closed shortly afterwards although for a short while, during the Great War, it was used to house prisoners of war. For the duration of the Great War it was in the hands of the army. The Highways and Works Department of the Council took it over in 1930 and demolished most of the interior buildings with the exception of the walls and the gatehouse. It remained as a storage depot until the late 1980s when it was restored and updated. In 1990, the site was re-opened as a business centre with what had been the exercise yards dominated by the restored Mrs Worley's fountain.

MRS WORLEY'S FOUNTAIN 2004 S2728k (Tom Doig)

All the parts of Mrs Worley's fountain were reassembled and it now stands in what was once the prison yard, a far cry from the grim exercise yard that was here in the years leading up to the First World War.

The Prison

The Grimston Road frontage is dominated by the Gaol's main gate. This has been used in a number of television programmes - it was the main gate to Slade Prison, home of Norman Stanley Fletcher played by Ronnie Barker in 'Porridge', and the entrance to the gaol in 'Within these Walls.' On either side of the gate are two houses - the larger was the residence of the Prison Governor whilst the smaller one was home to the Turnkey. In front of the gate, pointing directly at the visitor, is a huge iron cannon on a wooden wheeled carriage. It, and its reputed partner, were discovered during the excavation of the foundations of the new buildings and one was restored to stand guard at the entrance. It is said that its partner was thrown back into the footings of the yard and lies there today. Despite wide ranging speculation, nobody has convincingly explained the reasons for the existence of the cannons in St Albans. No doubt they were built for warfare as war is never far from us.

THE GATEWAY TO THE PRISON 2004
S2727k (Tom Doig)

Running eastwards from the Market Place, Victoria Street leads to the city railway station and Victoria Square. The name of Victoria Street has had a rather chequered career. At one time it was known as Shropshire Lane, occasionally Butts Lane, then from about 1835 Sweetbriar Lane and finally, in 1876, it became Victoria Street. Of all the streets in St Albans, Victoria Street arguably has the most interesting 19th century history. The Corporation had, in 1867, purchased the properties at the western end, where the road was narrow, to install new drains - this led to a new life.

Shortly after the renaming of Sweetbriar Lane, a privately owned public baths with a swimming pool, Turkish Bath and meeting room were built. For more than ten years the townspeople had been clamouring for public baths and in the face of an intransigent council, private enterprise gave them what they demanded. Sadly, demand and usage are not the same and within seven years they had closed and the building was taken over as barracks for the Salvation Army. Falling into disrepair, it was improved and converted into a Citadel in 1911. One of the foundation stones for the conversion was laid, on 4th February, by Councillor Samuel 'Sam' Ryder - a man whose name will be familiar to golf enthusiasts throughout the world. The original use of the building as a public bath can be seen, today, in the brown ceramic tiles of the unspoiled facade. The Salvation Army had a second centre at the junction of Camp and Campfield Roads. Here, from 1901, the SA Campfield Press printed 'War Cry' and 'Young Soldier' and there was a small factory making musical instruments. The premises were closed in 1992 and demolished to be replaced by a business centre.

By 1883, the Council had quickly realised their error in not purchasing the baths at a knock-down price and later bought the private baths by the Ver at Cottonmill Lane and then, in 1905, added an open air swimming pool - mixed swimming was not allowed until 1924.

THE SALVATION ARMY CITADEL 2004
S2721k (Tom Doig)

When the old public baths were converted into a Salvation Army Citadel, one of those who laid the foundation stone was Samuel Ryder, after whom golf's Ryder Cup is named.

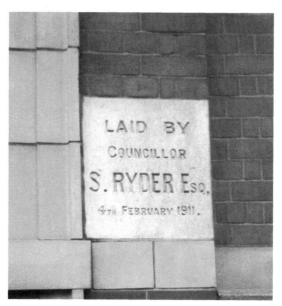

PLAQUE ON THE SALVATION ARMY CITADEL 2004
S2722k (Tom Doig)

A few doors west of the Salvation Army Citadel is the original Public Library and School of Science and Art. The corner stone was laid by the mayor, Mr J Chapple in April 1880 and the work completed in 1881. The cost was met by a public subscription of £2500 and 1d rate. The beautiful, and unspoiled, frontage is decorated with three

THE LIBRARY AND THE SCHOOL OF SCIENCE AND ART 2004 S2724k (Tom Doig)

The corner stone to the Public Library and School of Science and Art was laid in April 1880 by Mr Chapple, the Mayor. The building was completed at a cost of £2,500 in 1881.

relief terracotta roundels depicting Humphrey Davey (Science), William Hogarth (Art) and Francis Bacon (literature - did he write Shakespeare's plays?). Of the three, Bacon lived in St Albans, Hogarth visited St Albans and as for Davey - had he ever heard of St Albans? The old Library building, totally untouched, is now the premises of a group medical practice, the Maltings Surgery.

The great benefactor, Andrew Carnegie, was approached when it was clear that the original library was inadequate to meet the needs of the city. He generously agreed to underwrite the cost and the new Library, designed by Guilford Woudley, was built on the northern side of Victoria Street. The foundation stone was laid by Dr Eustace Lipscombe, mayor, on 27th October 1910 and on 10th October 1911, Dr Carnegie motored down from Scotland and, accompanied by the American ambassador, opened the Library. The latest St Albans library was opened by Diana, Princess of Wales in 1988, whilst Dr Carnegie's library became a public house, 'The Philanthropist and Firkin', and latterly, O'Neill's Irish theme bar. We can imagine that the Scottish Presbyterian Carnegie is turning in his grave.

Opposite the School of Science and Art was the Fire Station. A reference dated 1738 orders that 'two large fire engine be kept in the stable under the Town Hall' at the corner of Dagnal Street. Later, before 1819, the County Fire Office kept their engine in a barn at Adey & White's premises at The Brewery, between what is now Victoria Street and Chequer Street. The horses that pulled the engine were borrowed from the Brewery. A short poem recalls the excitement of the polished engine drawn by the snorting horses:

The engines thundered through the street,
Fire-hook, pipe, bucket all complete,
And torches glared, and clattering feet,
Along the pavement flew.

There was also a small fire engine house by the Abbey Gate House to the west of Romeland. In 1883, a fire station was built in Victoria Street on premises 'previously in the occupation of Mr Stebben.' It was used until the new station was constructed at Harpenden Road in 1964.

A little further down Victoria Street is the new Police Station. There had been a town police force since 1836 under the conditions of the Municipal Reform Act. When it was absorbed into the Hertfordshire constabulary in 1946, St Albans was one of the last independent forces in the country. The Police Station, housing six officers of varying ranks in 1851, was originally located behind the Town Hall and later adjacent to the site of the present Station. The new Police Station, part of the new civic centre complex which included City Hall, Law Courts and Health Centre, was designed by Sir Frederick Gibberd and built in 1966 on what had been the Society of Friends Quaker burial ground, in use between 1676 and 1869.

The Quakers were a force to be reckoned with in St Albans for, in 1797, Sir Frederick Eden tells us that, apart from the established church, 'there is one Anabaptist Chapel, 1 Calvanist chapel, 1 Quaker's meeting house and a congregation of Independents.' Opposite Bricket Road, the Tabernacle Baptist Church was opened in 1882 - it is now The Havana Club, a school of dance.

Did you know?

The County, later City, Museum was opened in 1899 on land given by Lord Spencer. Apart from artefacts relating to the history of St Albans it contains an internationally important collection of craftsmen's tools.

THE CITY MUSEUM 2004 S2714k (Tom Doig)

ST ALBANS ORDNANCE SURVEY MAP 1897

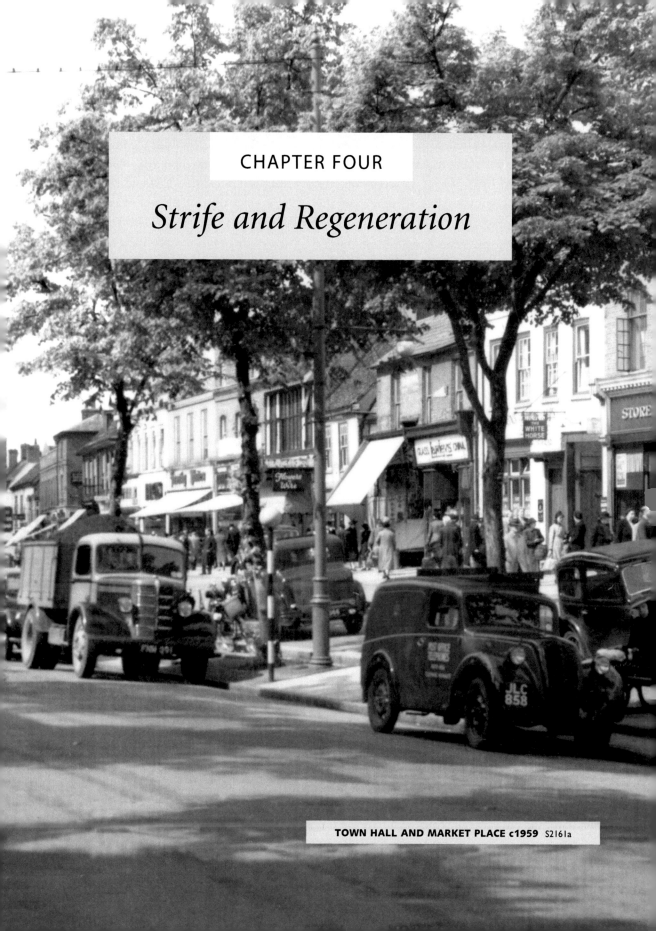

CHAPTER FOUR

Strife and Regeneration

TOWN HALL AND MARKET PLACE c1959 S2161a

IN 1905, the Northamptonshire boot makers marched through the town on their way to Parliament to lobby for fair wages. They were greeted by a delegation from the city's Boot and Shoe Operatives' Union and, after speeches and general flag waving, entertained to a sumptuous feast. A couple of months later, a similar 'small army' from Leicester were entertained. The Women's Suffrage Society advertised its forthcoming meetings in the Market Place by chalking times and dates on the pavement. In January 1911, the Town Council, never a group to avoid confrontation, made it a bye-law offence to write on the pavement. Of course, thousands turned out to see what all the fuss was about and the meetings were a great success!

During the 19th and early 20th centuries, Fishpool Street enjoyed a reputation as a place of sin and degradation. Many of the buildings were public houses, little more than beer shops, and disease was rife. In January 1902, there was an outbreak of smallpox in the town and, although Fishpool Street was spared, a simultaneous epidemic of scarlet fever claimed the life of a labourer lodging in one of the beer house-cum-rooming houses whilst the landlady, who was also infected, survived. Tony Billings, in his excellent 'St Albans Directory of Place Names', tells us that the houses on the north of the street were reputed to form the tuberculosis side whilst those on the south were known as the thrombosis side!

Back up Victoria Street just past the bridge over the railway is the turning into Alma Road named, with its nearby neighbour Inkerman

Road, after battles in the Crimean War. Both took place in the autumn of 1854 and it is safe to imagine that the houses were built shortly after. But we would be wrong, for it was originally called Cross Street and renamed Alma Road after the Crimean War. Alma Road cuts across from Victoria Street to the 'new' London Road and number fourteen was home to Arthur Melbourn-Cooper's Alpha Kinematograph Works. He produced a vast number of films including what is probably Britain's first animated film, 'Dreams of Toyland'. In 1908 he opened the Alpha Picture Palace in London Road. This 800 seater cinema was the first to be opened in St Albans; its replacement, built on the same site after fire destroyed the Picture Palace, as it was then known, was later the Capitol, later renamed the Odeon - when it closed in 1995, it was St Albans' last surviving cinema.

Also in Alma Road was the headquarters of the Trades and Labour Council. When a contingent of women from the north of England and from Scotland 'Hunger Marched' to Hyde Park in April 1930, they

Did you know?

In 1907, Arthur Melbourn-Cooper made a 'stop frame' animated film entitled 'Dreams of Toyland'. The opening sequence was filmed in St Peter's Street whilst the remainder was made in the studio at 14 Alma Road, the Alpha Kinematograph Works, close to the railway station.

were fed and lodged over night at the Council HQ in Alma Road. In a lighter vein, the Campaign for Real Ale had its offices in Alma Road on the corner of Oswald Road. Michael Hardman and Gordon Lees originally ran the Campaign from rooms above a bicycle shop in Victoria Street after the success of their first meeting on 20th November 1972 in the Farrier's Arms in Lower Dagnal Street. They moved to Alma Road in 1976 and then to Hatfield Road in 1995.

Alma Road meets London Road a few yards west of the point where London Road splits from Old London Road. The evolution of London Road is complex and often confusing. The first London Road was, of course, Watling Street. This certainly predated the Roman period and was still in use until the time of the Saxon abbot, Ulsinus. He diverted the road so that it ran up Holywell Hill, through Church Street and down Fishpool Street and the Sallypath. By the medieval period, the link between the bottom of Holywell Hill/St Stephen's Hill and Watling Street had been abandoned and the main road to London ran along Sopwell Lane into Old London Road. Tony Billings notes that in 1562, Sir Richard Lee diverted the medieval road to avoid his house, to run along the present Old London Road to the Toll Gate situated where the premises of Water's, Renault dealer, now stand. The 1851 census for Old London Road records that the toll-keeper was the wonderfully named Winsler Wise.

At the end of the 19th century, the straw hat trade was in a major decline and facing irresistible competition from foreign imports and the fashionable inclination to the felt hat. By 1907, the Victoria Street factories were closed and lying empty.

The great St Albans Pageant of July that year gave them a new, albeit short, lease of life when the costumes, banners and properties, designed by Robert Groves, head of the St Albans School of Art, were manufactured and stored in the long, silent workshops. For the duration of the celebration, Jefferson's old factory on the north-west corner became Pageant House and the late Claud Westell, who played the part of a young mourner at Queen Eleanor's funeral,

PAGEANT POSTER 1907 ZZZ01722

The 1907 St Albans Pageant was a great success and, with a cast of thousands, the whole city celebrated the people and their history. The front page of the programme depicted King Offa with the relics of St Alban.

recalled, 'One floor of the building resembled a medieval armoury, crammed as it was with swords of all sizes, shields, armour (plated and chained) and all the appurtenances of hand-to-hand fighting.' The Pageant was the brainchild of Charles Henry Ashdown and directed by Herbert Jarman, a Shakespearean actor-manager who later toured Australia, New Zealand and South Africa. After his appearances in the southern hemisphere,

AN OLD HAT FACTORY IN VICTORIA STREET 2004
ZZZ01717 (Tom Doig)

This shows a disused hat factory in Victoria Street. In the hey-day of the straw-plaiting industry, three of the corners of the junction were occupied by hat factories.

Jarman performed in New York in 1912. He always said, however, that the St Albans Pageant was his greatest success.

The Great War of 1914-18 took its toll on the population of St Albans and, apart from the main memorial at the north of St Peters Street, many of the communities erected their own smaller memorials to the local people who lost their lives. Outside 52 Fishpool Street, a small plaque bears a crucifix and lists the names of seven local men who paid the ultimate sacrifice. It was unveiled in April 1921 on the wall of the home of Private J A Peacock, 2nd Bedfordshire Regt, who was killed in action on 11th July 1916. This tablet is one of ten such memorials that were erected in St Albans. The others were at Albert Street, Bardwell Road, the High Street (next to Waxhouse Gate), Holywell Hill, Lower Dagnal Street, Orchard Street, Pageant Road, Sopwell Lane and Verulam Road. They all survive intact with the exception of Orchard Street, which has had the name plate removed, and Lower Dagnal Road, which has been defaced.

At the far end of St Peter's Street are both the city's war memorial and, of course, the church from which it takes its name. The war memorial was originally to have been erected where the Eleanor Cross previously stood. After a number of protests and lengthy discussion, it was agreed that it should be built on what had been a duck pond but by then was a small green known locally as the 'Tank Site.' A British Army tank was due to be displayed here but for bureaucratic reasons it failed to materialise. The memorial

HOUSE WITH MEMORIAL IN FISHPOOL STREET

2004 2702k (Tom Doig)

was dedicated on 22nd May 1921 by Ernest Watson, Mayor, and the Bishop of St Albans, Michael Furse. Made of Portland stone, it cost £372 raised by public subscription; the gardens and railings were provided by the city council. It records the names of 640 people from the city who gave their lives in the Great War including two families who lost three sons. It is said that, like the whole of the land, every family lost someone close in the Great War.

Along Victoria Street, between Upper Lattimore Road and a footpath leading through to Marlborough Gate in what was then known as Victoria Parade, stood Victoria Hall. In April 1934 this small meeting hall, trapped between small residences and work shops, was the scene of a dance organised in aid of the St Albans branch of the British Union Fascists, which attracted more than a hundred people, many dressed in black uniforms. One wonders how many of those who attended denied any knowledge of the event, five years later.

Behind Marlborough Gate, Marlborough House was the home of Samuel Ryder. Ryder was born in Preston, Lancashire in 1858, the son of a nurseryman. He attended Owen's College (now part of Manchester University) where, living near the ground at Old Trafford, he became a successful spin bowler. One of his first jobs was with a firm of Manchester Shipping Merchants. At some stage he was with a large London firm in the seed business. He was thirty-seven years of age when he came to St Albans in 1895. The St Albans Almanac for 1897 shows him living in a small terraced house at the top of Folly Lane. He lived there with his wife and daughter Lucy. Lucy remembered that her parents kept seeds in a shed in the garden and prepared catalogues and seed packets in the house. They carried a large clothes basket full of correspondence, chiefly seed catalogues, down to the Post Office a mile away. This was done each Friday night so that the catalogues would be in the hands of working men on Saturday afternoon when they would be enjoying their weekly half-day holiday. In 1903, the seed business moved to the rear of 27 Holywell Hill on the site of the Bull Inn.

ST PETER'S STREET 1921 70473p

ST PETER'S CHURCH AND THE WAR MEMORIAL 1921 70474p

Photographed a few weeks after the unveiling, the garden to the war memorial still has its covering of wreaths placed by families of those who were killed. The gentleman leaning over the rails may well be remembering his comrades who did not return to 'Blighty'.

THE WAR MEMORIAL, ST PETER'S STREET 2004
S2710k (Tom Doig)

The garden has been improved, the trees have grown and a tablet has been added to commemorate those who have been killed in action since the Great War. It still stands as a memorial to all who made the ultimate sacrifice for their country.

Having built up the seed packing business, eight years later he reconstructed the front premises facing Holywell Hill. In these buildings Ryder employed up to ninety girls packing seeds. With the help of his elder brother James, who had retired in March 1920 to study herbs and their medicinal value, Samuel then set up Heath & Heather Ltd to pack and market herbs. James had been a schoolmaster for forty years, chiefly in the slums of London. A start was made in July 1920 in a modest building in Albert Street. By March 1922, the company was operating from a former hat factory warehouse in

Dagnall Street, St Albans as well as a variety of warehouse facilities around the town. Sam's wife became Superintendent of Heath & Heather Ltd, and produced books on herbs. She also lectured throughout the country on the subject of 'Herbs and their Uses'. In 1925 the company's factory in Ridgmont Road was described as 'the largest retail herb warehouse in the world' and had a floor area of upwards of 24,000 square feet. Today Heath & Heather is part of the Holland and Barrett chain of shops.

During 1908 Samuel Ryder suffered a breakdown in health from which he was slow to recover. His friend, Rev Frank Wheeler, the Minister of Trinity Congregational Church, suggested a round of golf on the nearby nine-hole field on Cunningham Hill. He greeted the invitation with less than enthusiasm but reluctantly agreed. The rest of the story is the 'stuff of legends'. Samuel Ryder took to the game with a vengeance, joined the Verulam Golf Club and later founded the competition between British (later European) and American golfers for the world-famous Ryder Cup.

Did you know?

The Bull Inn was one of the largest inns in St Albans and described by a traveller in Tudor times as 'the greatest Inn I have seen in England.' It was visited by Queen Elizabeth who entertained there in 1577 and, more importantly, it was here that the remonstrance was signed confirming the trial of King Charles.

Ryder (who died in 1936) left his mark on the heritage of the town. There is hardly an early 20th century civic project in St Albans which was not influenced by Samuel Ryder. Marlborough House is now part of Loretto College but little appears to be known of the fate of Ryder's parrot which greeted visitors with a 'wobbly soprano' rendering of 'Onward Christian Soldiers'!

When the 1951 film 'The Magic Box' was made by John Boulting, Robert Donat, playing the part of William Friese-Greene, the pioneering film maker, ran out of the doorway of Violet Wedges shop in French Row. It appears on the screen for just a few seconds. Blink and you will miss it! The site is now occupied by the attractive and welcoming coffee shop, Puccinos. Part of this building on the eastern side of French Row was occupied by the 'Clock Tower Toilet Club' Nobody seems to be able to recall its function! French Row was a heavily used thoroughfare which was often blocked by tradesmen and delivery vehicles. It was eventually pedestrianised in 1976.

HOLLAND & BARRETT, ST PETER STREET 2004
S2725k (Tom Doig)

The St Peter Street branch of Holland & Barrett is a direct descendant of the company Heath and Heather, set up by Samuel Ryder of St Albans. The company has branches all over the country including this one in its home town. The frontage blends in with the traditional style of the area.

TRINITY CONGREGATIONAL CHURCH 2004
S2726k (Tom Doig)

Samuel Ryder contributed towards the cost of building Trinity Congregational Church on the corner of Victoria Street and Beacinsfield Road. Although damaged by fire in 1981, the URC remains one of the finest churches in St Albans.

ST ALBANS, FROM THE AIR 1967 AF67762

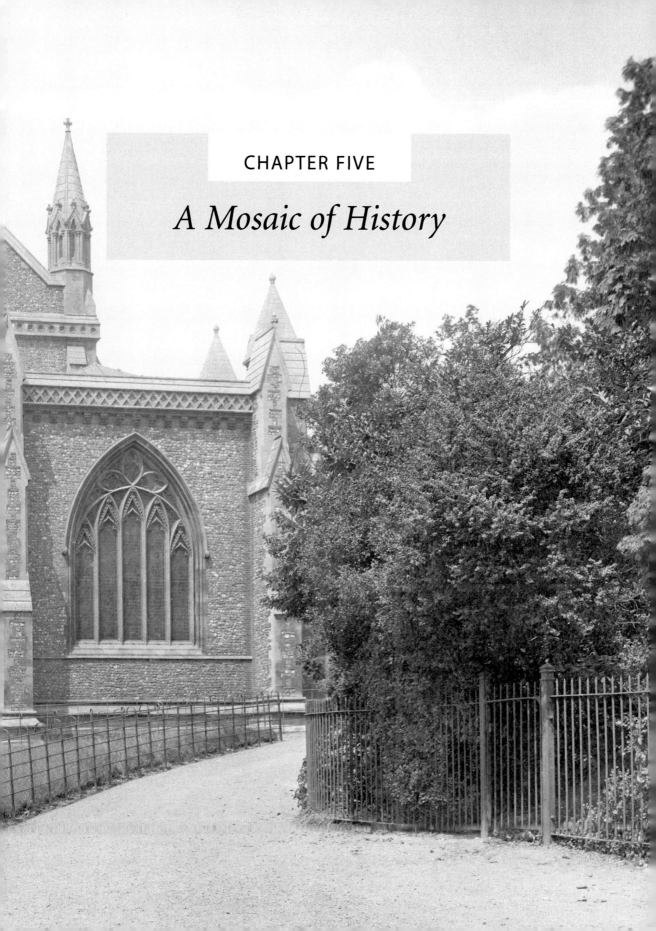

CHAPTER FIVE

A Mosaic of History

MANY OF the original buildings in St Peter's Street have been demolished and some of the fine houses have gone. The few that survive have been carefully maintained and give us an indication of what the main thoroughfare of St Albans looked like two hundred years ago.

It would be wrong to suggest that St Peter's Street has been spoiled. The beautifully maintained civic facilities blend into the traditional townscape and the new Civic Hall and Theatre are acceptable modern assets. St Albans is proud of its links with its twin towns and the shields of each is mounted high on the walls of the Council Offices: Worms, the home of Martin Luther, and Nevers, resting place of St Bernadette (and the home of the French motor racing grand prix at Magny-Cours!) as well as towns in Hungary and Italy. One or two of the 1960s buildings, particularly those not owned by the City or local businesses, are beginning to show their age and, sadly on occasions, spoil an otherwise, fine modern development. Secluded behind the buildings on the western side of St Peter's Street is a beautifully kept floral garden which is particularly welcome to the staff of the Civic Centre seeking a quiet spot for lunch. In one corner, almost hidden by the shubbery, is one of St Albans' fine pieces of community art. Unfortunately the sculptor is not acknowledged.

CIVIC CENTRE GARDEN 2004
S2713k (Tom Doig)

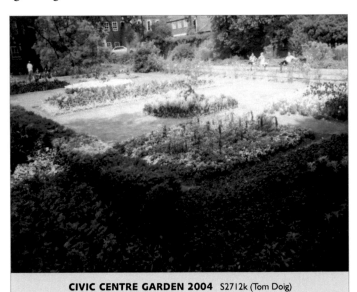

CIVIC CENTRE GARDEN 2004   S2712k (Tom Doig)

The Mosaic Mural

Another attractive work of art can be found up high above the St Peter's Street betting shop. So many visitors miss this beautiful mosaic mural. A quick upward glance shows that it traces the whole history of Verulamium and St Albans.

THE MOSAIC IN ST PETER'S STREET 2004

S2718k (Tom Doig)

Key: a) Verulamium Municipium - Verulamium was the first English city to be granted municipal rights under Roman rule.

b) The Sword and Eagle - representing the might of Rome.

c) II, IX & XX - the Roman Legions based at Verulamium.
II - Augusta.
IX - Hispania.
XX - Velaria Vitrix.

d) Offa's Cross - Offa was the King of Mercia.

e) Three Crosses - the three churches founded by St Ulsinus: St Peter's, St Michael's and St Stephen's.

f) The arms of the See of St Albans.

g) Arms of the City Council.

h) Novum Organum - Sir Francis Bacon's greatest work.

i) Some letters from 'The Boke of St Albans'.

j) Fleur de Lys - remembering the King of France's stay in St Albans.

k) Three shields: Margaret of Anjou, Earl of Warwick & de Vere Roses.

l) Tudor Rose.

m) Roses of Lancaster and York.

n) Three buildings - pilgrims flocked to sacred places in the Abbey and lodged in the town.

Some of the details in St Peter's Street should not be missed. Children love to stop a few houses along from the entrance to the civic facilities where one of the traditional doorways is guarded by a pair of cast iron owls, and who cannot fail to be fascinated by the blue tubular iron penny-farthing style bicycle racks where visitors' bikes can be chained.

Many of the modern buildings have been designed and built sympathetically and a number of the shops are outstanding in their effort to blend into the atmosphere of the City's main thoroughfare. Two stand out in particular - Holland & Barrett, health foods and natural products, whose antecedents have a close connection with the city, and the former Ottakar's bookshop premises seen in the photograph below.

CAST IRON OWL IN ST PETER'S STREET 2004
S2727k (Tom Doig)

Who could not be intrigued by this brown and white cast iron owl on the door step of a house in St Peter's Street?

ST PETER STREET 2004 S2716k (Tom Doig)

The frontage of the former Ottakar's bookshop in St Peter's Street in this 2004 photograph blends comfortably between two of the city's most beautiful buildings.

Opposite the former Ottakar's bookshop, on a triangular site stands the new Town Hall. The original Town Hall was located at the corner of Upper Dagnal Street, on the plot now occupied by W H Smith, until it was sold in 1831 for £914 10s. This had been unsuitable as the premises were also occupied by the Liberty Courthouse and the borough jailer. The entrance was blocked by animal pens on weekly market days and the Court proceedings were deafened by the clamour of trade outside the windows.

Although there had been a brief respite when the pig pens were moved away, the final solution had to wait until 1926 when the livestock market transferred to Drover's Way. The new Town Hall was built in 1829-1830 to a 1826 classical, almost Palladian, design by George Smith and opened in 1831. It stands on the site of the old 16th-century Clark's Almshouses which provided accommodation for three St Albans widows. Prior to the Almshouses, the Moot House stood here. The Town Hall also served as the Court House and the Dickensian prisoners' cells still survive in the undercroft.

In Bricket Road, the Crown Courts demonstrate the determination of the town's planners to ensure that new developments reflect the traditional style of the town. Built in 1993, the Crown Court has a Roman archway and is built of replica Roman brick. This is surmounted by an enormous Royal Coat of Arms over 15 feet across.

THE CROWN COURT 2004 S2723k (Tom Doig)

The new Crown Court was built in 1993 as part of the civic development. The Roman-style entrance way is surmounted with the Royal Arms.

Trinity Congregational Church, on the corner of Victoria Street and Beaconsfield Road, is one of the finest non-conformist churches in St Albans, and was constructed, with financial help from Samuel Ryder, in 1903. When the Congregational and Presbyterian Churches joined together in 1972, Trinity became the largest United Reform Church in St Albans. Trinity suffered a disastrous fire in July 1981 but after discussion as to its future, it was decided that it should be repaired and modernised. The work was carried out to a very high standard and today Trinity proudly stands a monument to St Albans' non-conformity.

On 22nd June 1877 the Roman Catholic Archbishop of Westminster, Cardinal Manning, laid the foundation stone of the Catholic Church of Saints Alban and Stephen on land donated by Major James Gape in London Road. Up to that time there had been no Roman Catholic church and Mass was sung in a cottage next to this new site whilst earlier, services had been held in a converted room over the White Hart Inn in Holywell Hill.

Although an abortive attempt to build a Catholic Church on the site of the failed Verulam Arms in Verulam Road had been started in 1848, the death in 1850 of the benefactor, Alexander Raphael, saw the end of the project. The half-constructed church was bought by Mrs Worley who underwrote the cost of its completion and saw it consecrated in 1859 as the Anglican Christ Church. It closed in 1974 and was converted to commercial units.

The main part of the new London Road Roman Catholic Church, which had been totally built by young lads overseen by a professional builder, was consecrated exactly a year later in 1879. It survived until 1905 when a replacement was built in Beaconsfield Road. The site is now a petrol and service station.

The red brick and terracotta County Museum (now the City Museum) was opened in 1899 on land given, for that sole purpose, by Lord Spencer. Amongst its treasures is the collection of traditional craftsmen's tools assembled by Raphael Salaman who was born at Barley in the north east of the county but lived most of his life at Harpenden. Next door, in an entirely different style of architecture, is the University of Hertfordshire's Faculty of Law, previously part of the College's Art Department although it continues to include the Margaret Harvey Gallery which displays the work of local artists. It reflects nicely with the ancient building and founding of the Grammar School and this modern continuance of education.

THE YARD OF THE WHITE HART c1875 ZZZ01725

Early meetings of the St Albans Roman Catholics were held in a room above the White Hart in Holywell Hill. It is possible that the services were conducted in the room over the arch.

The Peahen

At the top of London Road, on the left, stands the Peahen Hotel. The long 'burgage' plots, or 'backsides' that provided gardens and smallholdings for many of the houses in the town are still visible behind the Peahen and the White Hart, a short distance away. There is no evidence to support the tradition that King Henry VIII and Anne Boleyn were secretly married here after meeting clandestinely in Sopwell Lane at the bottom of the hill. With its new found importance on the corner of London Road, the Peahen soon absorbed the Woolpack next door and, in 1897, they were both rebuilt although some of the original medieval timbers and features survive. It was at the old Peahen, in 1819, that the inquest was held into the death of a coach traveller who was killed during a race through Redbourn between the Holyhead and Chester coaches when the Holyhead coach overturned. The two drivers (said to have been kept in irons for six months before their trial) were each sentenced to a year's imprisonment.

THE PEAHEN PUBLIC HOUSE 2004
S2729k (Tom Doig)

The Holy Well stood in the ground of the original Holywell House, home of the Marlborough and Spencer families and was hidden in a decorated grotto. It is said that water from the Well healed the battle wounds of Uther Pendragon, father of King Arthur.

The building of the London Road to meet the Market Place saw the decline of Holywell Hill and many of the original buildings, particularly those at the lower end. Traffic now flows along Watling Street into King Harry Lane where in earlier time it would have turned up St Stephen's Hill into the town.

On the other side of Holywell Hill to the railway station is the Abbey Theatre. The envy of many cities around the country, this was opened by the late Queen Mother in 1968. The Company of Ten had formed in 1934 after the closure of the County Theatre behind St Peter's Street and, through sterling effort, raised the funds to build a the new theatre of which it was justly proud.

Also at Abbey Hill Lane was the Silk Mill on the site of the Abbey corn mill. The silk mill operated between 1804 and 1905 by the Woollam family and was closed in 1938. It employed about 130 people at its height in the early 1900s when it was powered by steam. Part of the building was demolished and the remainder has now been converted into dwellings. The production of straw

Sir Francis Bacon

There are many remarkable features inside St Michael's Church - a Tudor altar table, a 15th century font, and an Jacobean oak pulpit (installed in line with a diocesan order of 1603), but the most interesting is the lifelike alabaster memorial to Sir Francis Bacon. 'Here sits Francis Bacon' in a thoughtful pose, maybe speculating where exactly in the church or churchyard he might be buried! Bacon asked, in his will, that he should be buried at St Michael's churchyard close to his mother but there is no record of this taking place nor has a location ever been found. His will, which was proved on 13th July 1627, makes no provision for his wife from whom he was estranged. It is possible that her final spite was for Bacon to be buried in an unmarked and unrecorded grave.

He had been called to take his seat in Parliament on a bitterly cold day in March 1626. On the return from Gray's Inn, a sudden fall of snow forced him to rest at Lord Arundel's house where he thought that he would take the opportunity to test his theory that frozen meat could be preserved as well as salted meat and he stuffed a chicken with fresh snow. He caught a chill and died at Highgate 'on April 9th 1626 in the early hours of Easter Sunday.'

A lawyer, courtier, essayist, statesman and philosopher, he was appointed Lord Chancellor and Baron Verulam in 1618 and later Viscount St Albans. Among his writings is one of the first science fiction books, 'New Atlantis,' which, unfortunately, he never finished.

ST MICHAEL'S CHURCH, FRANCIS BACON'S MEMORIAL c1885 18064
Sir Francis Bacon was buried in St Michael's Church. He died after experimenting with frozen food. Bacon stuffed a chicken with snow, but he caught a chill and died!

When Bacon died, his 'faithful friend and secretary' Sir Thomas Meautys erected the memorial to ensure that he was never forgotten. Bacon did not leave any sons and his direct male line died with him. Bacon's memorial is just that, a memorial, for nobody knows where he is buried although John Aubrey in his 'Brief Lives' says: 'This October,1681, it rang all over St Albans that Sir Harbottle Grimston, Master of the Rolles, had removed the Coffin of this most renowned Lord Chancellor to make roome for his owne to lye-in the vault there at St Michael's church.'

At his death Bacon was in difficult financial circumstances and claims against his estate ranged from £1,000 down to sixpence and included one for £80 from his 'butterwoman.' He did, however, leave £50 to the Church of St Michael. One wonders if the church ever received its inheritance.

In 1898, Lord Grimthorpe arranged for the rebuilding of St Michael's Church. Fortunately much of the original fabric survives and the full force of a 'Grimthorpe restoration' has not destroyed this beautiful church.

hats created a demand for the trimmings of lace, silk or cotton that were increasingly fashionable during the years leading up to the middle of the nineteenth century. This was probably one of the reasons for the prominence of the silk weaving business in St Albans.

We have toured the town of St Albans and seen it evolve from a Roman settlement to the thriving cathedral city of today. Francis Frith and his photographers recorded the past one hundred years or so of its evolution. Maybe we have been able to illustrate a few hundred years before that. But what of the thousand years after its founding? We can only imagine the shape, sounds and smell of the beautiful and welcoming city of St Albans.

> *When Verulam stood*
> *Saint Albans was a wood;*
> *But now Verulam's down*
> *St Albans is become a town.*
>
> *Anon.*

Did you know?

Outside the main building of St Michael's, but adjacent to the burial ground, once stood the parish house. Built during the 1600s, it later became the 'poor house' where the needy were given a bed and a meal. On its site was built the Sunday School and today, almost on the same spot, is the Parish Centre opened in 1973.

Did you know?

From St Michael's Church, the road to St Albans leads over Kingsbury Bridge - said to be the oldest surviving bridge in Hertfordshire. This was the site of the huge fishponds which were drained around AD880.

THE ABBEY 1921 70455

THE CATHEDRAL AND ABBEY CHURCH, THE EAST END 1921 70459

Despite extensive research, I have not been able to locate all copyright holders of the illustrations used in this book. Indeed, many of the drawings were executed a considerable time ago and probably no longer enjoy the protection of copyright. If I have infringed anyone's rights, please accept my apologies and understand that the fault lies at my door and not with the publishers.

ACKNOWLEDGEMENTS

My thanks are due to the staff at the Hertfordshire Archives and Local Studies Collection, Julia Skinner, Managing Editor at the Frith Book Company, who was incredibly understanding when the electronics failed, the staff at Flying Doctors computer service at Saffron Walden who worked miracles when I lost all the original script, Tony Billings for offering his photograph collection, the staff at Puccinos Coffee Shop in French Row, the manager of Topgeeza, Market Place, who introduced me to such interesting characters, and the Badge Guides of the City. Finally to my wife, Ann, who plied me with coffee and read both the original and the rescued scripts over and over and over again.

Of my reception by the people that I met in St Albans, I can only echo the words of Mrs Rose Smith who led the Women's Hunger March in 1930 when they lodged overnight in the Trades and Labour Council premises in Alma Road: 'The people here have been very kind to us. Indeed, their treatment has been the best we have ever experienced anywhere.'

Inevitably there are errors - these are all my own responsibility and I apologise for them. As Ford Maddox-Brown said of a guide to St Albans that he bought for a shilling during a visit to the city in 1854:

> *'We have spent six shillings getting here which is sheer madness*
> *in the present state of our prospects' and bought what was*
> *'certainly the silliest little book a fool ever penned, the most*
> *complete do that I was ever subjected to; fifty pages of the*
> *most complete vacuity that ever small-country-town-bred*
> *numbskull, without a shade of learning, ingenuity or imagination,*
> *could possibly have put into circulation.'*

BIBLIOGRAPHY

Morris, Kate, *St Albans Photographic Memories* Frith Book Company (2001)   ISBN 1-85937-341-0

Billings, Tony, *St Albans Directory* published by author (2002)   ISBN 0-9508803-6-1

Stratton, Ruth & Connell, Nicholas, *Haunted Hertfordshire* The Book Castle (2002) ISBN 1-903747-18-X

Wheeler, Anne, and Stevens, Tony, *Around St Albans* Tempus Publishing (2001)   ISBN 0-7524-2289-8

Corbett, James, *A History of St Albans* Phillimore (1997)   ISBN 1-86077-048-7

Corbett, James, *Picture Postcards of Old St Albans* MMA (1996)   ISBN 0-9522664-2-7

Mountfield, David, *Stages and Mail Coaches* Shire Publications (2003)   ISBN 0-7478-0554-7

Cussans, John Edwin, *History of Hertfordshire* (originally pub 1870) E Pub (1972)   ISBN 0-85409-833-X

Smith, J T, & North, M A , (ed.) *St Albans 1650-1700* Univ of Herts. (2003)   ISBN 0-9542189-3-0

Goose, Nigel, *St Albans & its region* (1851 Census analysis) Univ of Herts (2000)   ISBN 0-900458-83-6

Goodman, Alice, *The Street Memorials of St Albans Abbey Parish* SAHAAS (1987)   ISBN 0-901194-08-5

n a, *Memories of St Albans* True North Books (2000)   ISBN 1-903204-23-2

Flood, Susan, (ed.) *St Albans Wills 1471-1500* Hertfordshire Record Society (1993)   ISBN 0-9510728-8-9

Aubrey, John, *Brief Lives* (originally pub c1671) Secker & Warbury (1971)   ISBN 436 -12950-7

Branch Johnson, W, *Hertfordshire* Batsford (1970)   ISBN 7134-0067-6

Pelletier, Donald, (ed.) *St Albans Today*   no details in publication

Carrington, Beryl & Thresher, Muriel *The Ghost Book* (St Albans)   no details in publication

Osborne, Neil, *The Story of Hertfordshire Police* Hertfordshire Countryside (1969)   none

Alderman, H M, *A Pilgrimage in Hertfordshire* Trefoil Publishing (1931)   none

Mee, Arthur, *Hertfordshire* Hodder & Stoughton (1939)   none

Urwick, William, *Nonconformity in Herts* Hazell, Watson & Viney (1884)   none

Vale, Edmund, *The Mail Coach Men* Cassel (1960)   none

Hertfordshire Countryside magazine
Hertfordshire's Past Journal

Francis Frith
Pioneer Victorian Photographer

Francis Frith, founder of the world-famous photographic archive, was a multi-talented man. A devout Quaker and a highly successful Victorian businessman, he was philosophical by nature and pioneering in outlook. By 1855 he had already established a wholesale grocery business in Liverpool, and sold it for the astonishing sum of £200,000, which is the equivalent today of over £15,000,000. Now in his thirties, and captivated by the new science of photography, Frith set out on a series of pioneering journeys up the Nile and to the Near East.

He was the first photographer to venture beyond the sixth cataract of the Nile. Africa was still the mysterious 'Dark Continent', and Stanley and Livingstone's historic meeting was a decade into the future. The conditions for picture taking confound belief. He laboured for hours in his wicker dark-room in the sweltering heat of the desert, while the volatile chemicals fizzed dangerously in their trays. Back in London he exhibited his photographs and was 'rapturously cheered' by members of the Royal Society. His reputation as a photographer was made overnight.

By the 1870s the railways had threaded their way across the country, and Bank Holidays and half-day Saturdays had been made obligatory by Act of Parliament. All of a sudden the working man and his family were able to enjoy days out, take holidays, and see a little more of the world.

With typical business acumen, Francis Frith foresaw that these new tourists would enjoy having souvenirs to commemorate their days out. For the next thirty years he travelled the country by train and by pony and trap, producing fine photographs of seaside resorts and beauty spots that were keenly bought by millions of Victorians. These prints were painstakingly pasted into family albums and pored over during the dark nights of winter, rekindling precious memories of summer excursions. Frith's studio was soon supplying retail shops all over the country, and by 1890 F Frith & Co had become the greatest specialist photographic publishing company in the world, with over 2,000 sales outlets, and pioneered the picture postcard.

Francis Frith had died in 1898 at his villa in Cannes, his great project still growing. By 1970 the archive he created contained over a third of a million pictures showing 7,000 British towns and villages.

Frith's legacy to us today is of immense significance and value, for the magnificent archive of evocative photographs he created provides a unique record of change in the cities, towns and villages throughout Britain over a century and more. Frith and his fellow studio photographers revisited locations many times down the years to update their views, compiling for us an enthralling and colourful pageant of British life and character.

We are fortunate that Frith was dedicated to recording the minutiae of everyday life. For it is this sheer wealth of visual data, the painstaking chronicle of changes in dress, transport, street layouts, buildings, housing and landscape that captivates us so much today, offering us a powerful link with the past and with the lives of our ancestors.

Computers have now made it possible for Frith's many thousands of images to be accessed almost instantly. The archive offers every one of us an opportunity to examine the places where we and our families have lived and worked down the years. Its images, depicting our shared past, are now bringing pleasure and enlightenment to millions around the world a century and more after his death. For further information visit: **www.francisfrith.com**

FRITH PRODUCTS & SERVICES

Francis Frith would doubtless be pleased to know that the pioneering publishing venture he started in 1860 still continues today. Over a hundred and forty years later, The Francis Frith Collection continues in the same innovative tradition and is now one of the foremost publishers of vintage photographs in the world. Some of the current activities include:

INTERIOR DECORATION

Today Frith's photographs can be seen framed and as giant wall murals in thousands of pubs, restaurants, hotels, banks, retail stores and other public buildings throughout the country. In every case they enhance the unique local atmosphere of the places they depict and provide reminders of gentler days in an increasingly busy and frenetic world.

PRODUCT PROMOTIONS

Frith products are used by many major companies to promote the sales of their own products or to reinforce their own history and heritage. Frith promotions have been used by Hovis bread, Courage beers, Scots Porage Oats, Colman's mustard, Cadbury's foods, Mellow Birds coffee, Dunhill pipe tobacco, Guinness, and Bulmer's Cider.

GENEALOGY AND FAMILY HISTORY

As the interest in family history and roots grows world-wide, more and more people are turning to Frith's photographs of Great Britain for images of the towns, villages and streets where their ancestors lived; and, of course, photographs of the churches and chapels where their ancestors were christened, married and buried are an essential part of every genealogy tree and family album.

FRITH PRODUCTS

All Frith photographs are available Framed or just as Mounted Prints and Posters (size 23 x 16 inches). These may be ordered from the address below. Other products available are - Address Books, Calendars, Jigsaws, Canvas Prints, Postcards and local and prestige books.

THE INTERNET

Already ninety thousand Frith photographs can be viewed and purchased on the internet through the Frith websites and a myriad of partner sites.

For more detailed information on Frith products, look at this site:
www.francisfrith.com

See the complete list of Frith Books at: www.francisfrith.com
This web site is regularly updated with the latest list of publications from The Francis Frith Collection. If you wish to buy books relating to another part of the country that your local bookshop does not stock, you may purchase on-line.

For further information, trade, or author enquiries please contact us at the address below:
The Francis Frith Collection, Unit 6, Oakley Business Park, Wylye Road, Dinton, Wiltshire SP3 5EU.
Tel: +44 (0)1722 716 376 Fax: +44 (0)1722 716 881 Email: sales@francisfrith.co.uk

---

See Frith products on the internet at www.francisfrith.com

FREE PRINT OF YOUR CHOICE
CHOOSE A PHOTOGRAPH FROM THIS BOOK

+ £3.80 POSTAGE

Mounted Print
Overall size 14 x 11 inches (355 x 280mm)

TO RECEIVE YOUR FREE PRINT

Choose any Frith photograph in this book

Simply complete the Voucher opposite and
return it with your remittance for £3.50 (to cover
postage and handling) and we will print the
photograph of your choice in SEPIA (size 11 x 8
inches) and supply it in a cream mount ready to
frame (overall size 14 x 11 inches).

Order additional Mounted Prints
at HALF PRICE - £12.00 each (normally £24.00)

If you would like to order more Frith prints
from this book, possibly as gifts for friends and
family, you can buy them at half price (with no
additional postage costs).

Have your Mounted Prints framed

For an extra £20.00 per print you can have your
mounted print(s) framed in an elegant polished
wood and gilt moulding, overall size
16 x 13 inches (no additional postage required).

IMPORTANT!

❶ Please note: aerial photographs and photographs
with a reference number starting with a "Z" are not Frith
photographs and cannot be supplied under this offer.

❷ Offer valid for delivery to one UK address only.

❸ These special prices are only available if you use this
form to order. You must use the ORIGINAL VOUCHER on
this page (no copies permitted). We can only despatch
to one UK address.

❹ This offer cannot be combined with any other offer.

As a customer your name & address will be stored by Frith but not sold or rented
to third parties. Your data will be used for the purpose of this promotion only.

Send completed Voucher form to:

The Francis Frith Collection,
19 Kingsmead Business Park, Gillingham,
Dorset SP8 5FB

Voucher for **FREE**
and Reduced Price
Frith Prints

*Please do not photocopy this voucher. Only the original is valid,
so please fill it in, cut it out and return it to us with your order.*

Picture ref no	Page no	Qty	Mounted @ £12.00	Framed + £20.00	Total Cost £
		1	Free of charge*	£	£
			£12.00	£	£
			£12.00	£	£
			£12.00	£	£
			£12.00	£	£
			£12.00	£	£

*Please allow 28 days
for delivery.
Offer available to one
UK address only*

* Post & handling £3.80

Total Order Cost £

Title of this book . . . .

I enclose a cheque/postal order for £ . . . .
made payable to 'The Francis Frith Collection'

OR please debit my Mastercard / Visa / Maestro card,
details below

Card Number:

Issue No (Maestro only):   Valid from (Maestro):

Card Security Number: Expires:

Signature:

Name Mr/Mrs/Ms . . . .

Address . . . .

. . . .

. . . .

. . . . Postcode . . . .

Daytime Tel No . . . .

Email . . . .

Valid to 31/12/16

Free Print – see overleaf

Can you help us with information about any of the Frith photographs in this book?

We are gradually compiling an historical record for each of the photographs in the Frith archive. It is always fascinating to find out the names of the people shown in the pictures, as well as insights into the shops, buildings and other features depicted.

If you recognize anyone in the photographs in this book, or if you have information not already included in the author's caption, do let us know. We would love to hear from you, and will try to publish it in future books or articles.

An Invitation from The Francis Frith Collection to Share Your Memories

The 'Share Your Memories' feature of our website allows members of the public to add personal memories relating to the places featured in our photographs, or comment on others already added. Seeing a place from your past can rekindle forgotten or long held memories. Why not visit the website, find photographs of places you know well and add YOUR story for others to read and enjoy? We would love to hear from you!

www.francisfrith.com/memories

Our production team

Frith books are produced by a small dedicated team at offices near Salisbury. Most have worked with the Frith Collection for many years. All have in common one quality: they have a passion for the Frith Collection.

Frith Books and Gifts

We have a wide range of books and gifts available on our website utilising our photographic archive, many of which can be individually personalised.

www.francisfrith.com